EGG PRODUCTION AND INCUBATION

EGG PRODUCTION AND INCUBATION

Prepared by
The Game Conservancy's Advisory Service

Published by
THE GAME CONSERVANCY
Fordingbridge
Hampshire SP6 1EF
Telephone No: (0425) 652381

First published in 1993

Printed and bound in Great Britain by
BAS Printers Limited, Over Wallop, Hampshire

CONTENTS

About this book

EGG PRODUCTION AND INCUBATION

ABOUT THIS BOOK

This Guide forms a part of The Game Conservancy's highly respected collection which covers the full range of game management topics. This is in some senses the first volume in a three part series, the subsequent two being Gamebird Rearing (No. 8) and Gamebird Releasing (No. 10). The book aims to give a broad overview of the various techniques of the production and incubation of pheasant and partridge eggs. It is essentially a practical guide which is designed to give the novice the confidence to go ahead and produce first class day old chicks using any of the standard incubation machines. At the same time, it aims to give guidance on other less common techniques, including the use of broody hens.

CHAPTER ONE

Why Rear Gamebirds?

Artificial rearing of pheasants and partridges has become such a "normal" part of game management over the last forty years that many people have almost forgotten that it is not the only route to successful shooting. Although reared pheasants made their contribution as early as a century ago, the large majority of the gamebirds which were shot by the Victorian and Edwardian sportsmen were truly wild bred birds. A combination of less intensive farming and highly efficient keepering meant that wild partridges and pheasants thrived as never before (or since). This was in many ways a happy accident, for while the predator control which the keepers carried out was fully deliberate, the other factors which combined to produce this abundance of wild game were very much outside the keeper's direct control.

Fortuitously our ancestors had hit upon what The Game Conservancy's research scientists now call "the three legged stool". They were in a situation in which the three basic life requirements of gamebirds were produced *in balance* with one another. In common with any other organism, a gamebird needs a good habitat, food, and freedom from excessive predation.

At the time of those great game shoots, the British landscape had over much of its area a kind of mixed farming with plentiful hedges and small woods which provided ideal pheasant and partridge habitat. At the same time farm crops were comparatively full of weeds, and the insects which depend on them and which in turn provide the correct food for game chicks. With no noticeable winter food shortages and heavy predation control, the living for gamebirds was good.

Today we have lost that special balance in all but a few places. Hedges and spinneys have gone, so there are less "gamebird homes". Farming is much more intensive and productive, so there is much less chick food, and keepers are far fewer, so there is much more

1

pressure on gamebirds from common predators like magpies and foxes. As a consequence, the part played in our sport by truly wild pheasants and partridges has sadly declined.

This said, there are still areas where wild birds provide all the sport that is required, and *those areas could be much extended given proper attention to all three aspects of the three legged stool.* In many senses, the key factor in this equation is The Game Conservancy's conservation headlands technique. If the outer six metres of cereal fields are selectively sprayed in the ways which this scheme recommends, the key weeds and insects return, and gamebird chick survival can return to its old level. Once this is combined with good habitat conservation and efficient control of key predators at nesting time, gamebird populations really can climb back to realistic sporting levels.

Incubation the old way. Even in the heyday of wild game shoots, hand-reared birds played their part.

2

Meanwhile, the hand-reared bird still has its part to play. Even when wild game management was at its peak, pheasants were being reared by keepers all over the country. This both supplemented numbers and helped to iron out the variations in the wild birds' breeding success in different seasons.

Since then overall demand for shooting has increased, and the hand-reared pheasant has filled the breach – providing good sport throughout the country. This is especially important when one realises that very large areas of the wetter west and north could never sustain a wild population of pheasants or partridges in sufficient numbers to allow driven shooting. A combination of unsuitable climate and mainly grassland agriculture simply will not support these large breeding populations. However, the landscape is often very suitable for the holding and showing of birds, and much good conservation work is done in their name.

Thus hand-reared birds will remain an important element of the sport on the majority of Britain's shoots for the foreseeable future. A fortunate few will continue to be able to rely entirely on wild birds, and many more will be able to encourage natural breeding and reap a reward from it, while supplementing with birds from

Hand-reared pheasants will probably continue as Britain's principal gamebird for some time to come.

the brooder house, but it is probably true to say that the hand-reared pheasant will continue as the principal gamebird for some time to come.

Dangers of Reared Birds

Recent research by The Game Conservancy has reinforced the view, widely held by many keepers, that hand-reared birds do not usually breed well in the wild. The full causes are not yet understood and are at present the subject of intensive research at The Game Conservancy. There are also variations between species, but this does not detract from the basic truth that a purely wild hen is more likely to rear a brood successfully on the shoot than a hand-reared one left over after the shooting season.

There is thus a real danger in areas which have healthy stocks of wild birds, and particularly of grey partridges, that the release of hand-reared birds will harm the population. This can arise in three main ways. Firstly, if hand-reared birds compete for limited breeding territories they could then fail to raise a brood where a wild bird would have succeeded. Secondly, high populations of hand-reared birds, which can be particularly prone to predation anyway, could encourage predators to hunt for game and increase losses to wild birds too. Thirdly, there is the effect of shooting pressure. When hand-reared birds are released it is "normal" to expect to shoot around 40% by the end of the season, and some well run shoots achieve much higher results. Wild populations cannot normally sustain more than 30% cropping. It is rarely possible to tell between the wild and reared birds of the same species under shooting conditions (indeed, if it were possible, the reared element would not be up to the required standard). Thus, in taking a "fair" harvest of the released birds, there is a risk of overshooting the wild population.

For all these reasons it pays to think long and hard before you plan to release any birds. If you are doing it to conserve wild game, you are almost certainly making a mistake. You would be better off to concentrate on a balanced improvement of "the three legged stool". However, if your plan is simply to provide good sport in an area where nature does not provide sufficient, releasing probably

4

is the way forward. Even so, do not lose sight of the fact that your aim is still the production of birds which are indistinguishable in their performance from fully wild birds. You will need good habitat and a commitment to good management. Gamebird rearing is not an end in itself, but rather a means to an end. That end should be good quality shooting and the conservation of the countryside.

Home Produced Eggs . . . A Good Idea?

Having established that releasing gamebirds is a good plan for your shoot, you still have decisions to make. Many shoots rush into catching up hens and home production of a new stock without thinking about whether this is the best policy for them. This is a great mistake in that it can lead to a heavy drain on limited resources without producing the best results. It pays to stop and think about the choices before you go in "both feet first". Restocking policies can fall into a wide range of categories of which the following, or a combination, are all possibilities:

1. Buy in poults and release
2. Buy in day olds, rear and release
3. Buy in eggs, hatch, rear and release
4. Pen hens, produce eggs, hatch, rear and release
5. Pen hens, send eggs for custom hatching or swap eggs for chicks, and home rear
6. Pen hens, swap eggs for poults
7. Catch surplus hens and send to game farm in exchange for poults.

All of these policies have their merits on different shoots, and you should give careful consideration to which suits you best. Over the last twenty years there has been a change of emphasis which could help to guide the "average" shoot. This has been that the proportion of smaller shoots which incubate their own eggs has declined. There are many reasons for this, but two in particular deserve mention. One is that large game farms can manage to make "economies of scale" so that their incubation cost per egg is far below that of the smaller unit. The other is that the "artificial" environment of an incubator is difficult to maintain. Larger incubators hold their temperature and humidity more readily than small ones. As a consequence, hatch rates from big units are often higher. This again gives the game farmer the edge in economic terms over the smaller home producers. Thus many shoots which used to incubate their own eggs have changed policy in recent years. Rather than replace an old and tired incubator with an expensive new machine, they have taken to sending their eggs for custom hatching, or swapping them for day olds from the game farm. This can make life much easier, but does carry a risk of importing disease.

Another factor in this decision is the economics of rearing. Weekly hatches from a relatively small stock can lead to small numbers of day olds which do not properly fill a brooder hut. As a consequence the equipment, heating and labour cost per bird is high.

On the other hand, for those on smaller D-I-Y shoots to whom incubation and rearing is an absorbing hobby as well as part of the management, home incubation is the answer. It may be that such shoots only wish to release a hundred birds, and that a couple of small table-top incubators are all that is needed for them to produce their birds at minimum cost. Such small batches could also be incubated and reared under broody hens. Either way, this relies on those who do the work not counting the cost in terms of time. In such small operations this will inevitably be high.

Many other shoots fall between these two categories. They have good incubators at hand, and all the facilities in terms of staff and equipment available. In this case, again, the wisest use of resources is to produce eggs and incubate at home. This only applies if the work involved does not detract from other more important aspects of the keepering. No gamekeeper can be expected to be in two places, doing two jobs, at one time. Those who are tied to a laying pen, incubators and a rearing field cannot possibly carry out as much predator control and habitat improvement work as those who are free from these duties. Also, if catching up enough stock to fill the laying pens means removing every last hen from the shoot, wild production is bound to be low, whatever the potential of the ground and the year.

In the end, each shoot will need to make its own policy decision on this question. The important point to make is that all factors must be weighed together and the best choice for the particular

A pheasant poult for release is worth about six times the value of an egg.

shoot taken. Just because it is not the same as that taken next door does not mean that it is wrong. Indeed, since the next door shoot is a different enterprise, another strategy is almost certainly required there.

In making the right decision, it will help to have a fair idea of the relative value of egg, chick and poult in economic terms. Monetary values change with time, but taking a pheasant egg as having a value of one unit, a day old chick is worth about two units, and a six week poult six units. In general it is also the case that small scale operations are rarely truly viable. The combination of economy of scale and the reduced need for long term egg storage between settings makes larger operations far more practical.

7

Scales of Production

Assuming that there is no limitation due to incubator capacity or equipment availability, the factor which dictates the size of laying stock required is the final number of poults needed for restocking. Thus, in deciding what breeding stock you want, your first question should really be "How much shooting do we expect?" Each shoot will have its own characteristics which affect the return on released birds, but a good basic figure to work on for both pheasants and partridges is that about 40% of the birds released will find their way into the bag. It must be confessed that this figure is perhaps a slight over-estimate for grey partridges, mainly because the Guns seem to have more trouble hitting them than either redlegs or pheasants! On the other hand, many well keepered shoots achieve a higher level of return, sometimes reaching over 50%.

For most shoots, therefore, 100 poults released should result in about 40 birds shot. Working back from this, given good management on the rearing field, it should be possible to rear over 90% of day olds, whether partridges or pheasants, to release age. There will, of course, be variations from batch to batch, and most groups should exceed 95%, but odd disasters with accidents or disease inevitably erode the overall figure. Working back from this point, pheasants and partridges differ significantly enough in egg production and hatch value to demand that separate calculations are needed for the three species.

a) *Pheasants*

It is a well known truth that the keeper expects to find his first pheasant egg in the laying pen on All Fools Day! However, very few pheasants start to lay quite so early, and it is probably fair to say that the season only really gets fully under way in the middle of April. In the six weeks to the end of May an average hen will lay about thirty eggs (five eggs per week) and this can be increased to perhaps 42 by 21 June (the very latest date by which eggs should be set if birds are to mature in time for the shooting season).

Artificial incubation of pheasant eggs rarely produces as high a hatch as in nature, and about 65%–75% can probably be taken as a usual level on the average estate. Thus Table 1 can be used to calculate the stock needed. It is based on production of 1000 poults for ease of calculation, with 67% hatching and a little over 90% rearing. It can be used for any number, although other calculations will be needed for very small batches.

Table 1: The relationship between pheasant stock and production	
Stage	Number
6 week poults	1000
Day olds	1100
Eggs	1600
Hens (6 week cycle to late May : 18 poults/hen)	54
Hens (8 week cycle mid June : 25 poults/hen)	40
Wintering hens	50–60
Wintering cocks	8–12

The 67% hatch given above assumes *fresh* eggs are used. Pheasant eggs over about eight days old lose their viability quite quickly. This combined with the lower hatch rate mentioned for small incubators means that those who require a single batch of say 100 poults for release must allow for the penning of more hens than the table would indicate. In practice a single pen with less than nine or ten hens is probably a very uneconomic exercise anyway. The problem of deterioration in storage can be quite significant on larger shoots too. This is because release of mixed age poults in the same pen often leads to bullying of the smaller birds. As a result, a shoot with only a few release pens will have trouble in managing the release of weekly batches. A good plan here is to pen a larger flock of hens, hatch early birds, and release the laying stock in May, as soon as they are no longer needed.

b) *Redleg Partridges*

Redlegs start to lay rather later than pheasants – usually about the third week of April, but again they reach a peak production of about five eggs per week. Taking mid June as the latest date for setting if birds are to be mature in time for the shooting season, a maximum of about 30 eggs per hen can be expected. First year birds do not achieve this kind of productivity. Indeed, studies at The Game Conservancy have shown that production increases annually as birds grow older for at least the first three years.

Egg production by first year birds is also governed by when they were hatched. Any hen hatched after mid July is unlikely to produce any eggs at all in its first season. Birds for breeding stock should therefore be selected from June hatches, in which case ten eggs per hen in the first season is a reasonable expectation. Second year birds should produce about 25 eggs, with the maximum of 30 from three years and older hens.

Another factor which affects production is the penning system; birds in pair boxes usually produce slightly more eggs than those flock mated. It is probably fair to take an average production of 25 eggs per adult hen as a basis for calculation.

Hatch rates with redlegs are normally rather better than from pheasants, and 80% is probably a reasonable average given good management. On this basis each hen should be expected to produce 20 day olds, and therefore 18 poults for release. Table 2 gives a good

Table 2: The relationship between redleg partridge stock and production	
Stage	Number
Poults (say 8 weeks)	1000
Day olds	1100
Eggs (80% hatch)	1400
Hens (18 poults/hen)	56
Wintering hens	60–65
Wintering cocks (pairs)	60–65
Wintering cocks (flock)	15–20

guide. It is again based upon 1000 birds produced, although this is likely to be more than most shoots will need.

The problem over storage mentioned for pheasants is not so serious for redleg partridges. Given good conditions, eggs up to three weeks old retain their viability well. Also, partridges are normally released in "covey" sized groups rather than the large central pen system used for pheasants. So small scale producers will have less problem in obtaining the full potential of their laying stock, and will not need to pen extra birds in the same way to obtain batches of equal ages.

c) *Grey Partridges*

Grey partridges are different again. Once in full lay, as for the other species, five eggs per week is probably a good average. They usually start to lay a little earlier than redlegs, around mid April, and can be expected to produce about 35 eggs per hen by mid June. In common with redlegs, their hatchability is usually fairly high, at around 80%. However, storage problems similar to those for pheasants are applicable. Also, greys are more "difficult" to rear, and loss rates up to release age are often higher.

The Game Conservancy carried out experiments with the retention of adult breeders for subsequent seasons, but results were not good. Average egg production was generally a little lower, and the viability of eggs and chicks often noticeably poorer. On this basis, the best policy seems to be to retain a new young breeding stock each year.

Grey partridges are also very aggressive birds and cannot be successfully flock mated. It is therefore essential to keep enough cock birds each year to match the number of hens overwintered. Table 3, again based on producing 1000 poults, should give a good guide to stock requirements.

Again, with small coveys as the normal release system, staggered ages at hatch should not pose a serious problem. However, eggs should be set at weekly intervals, which poses problems for small producers in filling brooder units. For this reason, bantam rearing is a particularly suitable system for grey partridges. Otherwise small

11

Table 3: The relationship betweeen grey partridge stock and production

Stage	Number
Poults (say 8 weeks)	1000
Day olds	1200
Eggs (80% hatch)	1500
Pairs (24 poults/pair)	43
Wintering hens	50
Wintering cocks	50

scale producers will be wise to pen a comparatively large stock for a short period to produce sensible sized batches for rearing, or alternatively take the cheaper option of buying in day olds.

SECTION B.   EGG PRODUCTION

CHAPTER TWO

What is an Egg?

The avian egg is a remarkable structure which enables the embryo to develop within its own protective environment outside the parent hen in a nest and, in addition, in a suitable artificial incubator that attempts to mimic the nest and movement of the hen. Whether or not a fertile egg hatches into a viable chick depends on numerous factors, some outside our influence but others within our control.

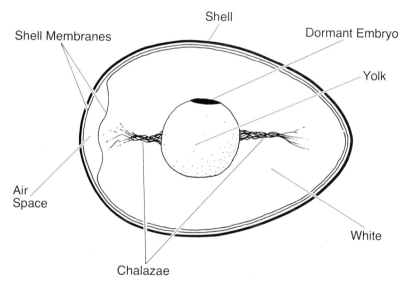

Figure 1. The structure of a new laid Egg.

The hard calcareous shell with its special egg shape and consequent high strength affords considerable protection to the developing embryo against the outside world. However, since the eggshell is fixed in size it can only contain a certain amount of nutrients provided by the hen for the developing embryo to utilize and grow, and eventually to hatch into an independent chick. Should any egg be marginal or deficient in quality no supplementary nutrients can be added once the egg is formed to help the embryo develop and hatch.

Air containing the oxygen necessary for respiration passes in through the numerous pores permeating the shell, while the subsequently produced carbon dioxide is passed out. Water is also continually lost as vapour through the pores, leaving an increasing airspace between the two main layers of the shell membrane in the large end for the hatching chick to break into and change over to lung breathing before the egg is finally chipped open. The system provides for interchange between oxygen and carbon dioxide through a special blood vascular structure lining most of the shell and membrane during incubation. The three layered porous non-living shell membrane immediately lining the inside of the shell forms a sac to contain the clear proteinaceous albumen, or egg white, and other components. Together with the shell, the various components of the egg combine to provide an excellent defence against disease and rotting microbes. On occasion, however, especially with poor handling, hygiene or hatchery practice, this defence can break down.

Floating in the middle of the albumen, and held in place by flexible protein strands or chalazae, is the ovum contained in its own sac; this is commonly called the yolk and contains large amounts of fats, some protein, carbohydrates and other essential nutrients. These groups of nutrients, contained inside what is effectively one extremely large cell, are laid down in the ovary prior to the shedding of the ovum and fertilisation and it is important that the hen is properly fed to ensure that she can deposit adequate quantities of high quality nutrients in the yolk.

Once fertilisation of the currently shed ovum has occurred at the top of the oviduct the yolk continues on a slow passage down this tubular organ. First of all it is coated with several layers of albumen, followed further down by the membranes to make a sac. The inner layer of the shell is next attached to the membranes followed by the outer components of the calcareous shell. As the shell is laid down holes or pores are left to provide a route for the gaseous exchange necessary for the life of the embryo. The eggs' shape, number and distribution are characteristic of the species, but can be modified by factors such as health and nutrition. Studies have shown that some failed eggs have, for instance, fewer pores than normal. Colour is next laid on the shell and finally the layer known as the cuticle, which contains a series of small cracks mostly related to the position of the pore exits. By the time that the egg is laid it will have been at body temperature for about one day and the single fertilised cell will have become many thousand cells. The egg then cools, stopping development until the egg is set in an incubator or under a hen. Any excessive storage temperature above about 70°F (21°C) allows development to continue, albeit slowly, but this has an adverse effect on the long term development and viability of the embryo.

The production of an egg is a delicate process. Low standards of husbandry, such as poor food and water supplies, are likely to result in ill-health, disease and stress to the bird. In turn the ovary and oviduct's ability to form an egg of good quality, suitable for hatching in incubators, can be adversely affected.

Quality production means attention to detail. Keep everything clean.

While potentially any hen can produce eggs, a high hatch rate of quality chicks to go in the rearing unit can only be achieved by careful attention to detail. Avoid cutting corners at any stage. Diligence should be given to quality laying stock and their penning, feeding and watering. Eggs should be carefully handled, sanitised and stored, while clean, hygienic conditions in the setter, hatcher and hatchery should always prevail. The production of quality day olds must not be thought of as a short term activity in the spring, but as a year-round procedure on which to base a successful rearing and release programme.

Quality of Breeding Stock

It should go without saying that only best quality birds should be used for breeding. Poor birds with any sign of injury or disease should be rejected. Where there is a history of disease this can be checked for in various ways by your veterinary surgeon and any cases treated or culled. Since relatively small numbers of birds are involved, on veterinary advice, individual injection with an appropriate long-acting drug might be considered suitable treatment. Periodic deworming of the flock via the food can in some instances be valuable, especially before the birds are moved to a new pen, and some products may be given to individual birds on veterinary advice.

Having discarded any obviously poor birds, the next question is what birds to select and keep. It is accepted that two year old pheasants tend to start laying earlier than first year birds and that they produce better quality eggs. They are also less likely to take to the vice of egg eating. In the long term, however, there is a serious risk of avian tuberculosis with losses and problems in the future. This disease is best controlled by using known young birds whenever possible and penning them on clean ground that has been free of birds for two or more years. When the exact age of the birds is known (established by tagging or otherwise), they should preferably have been hatched in May. Late hatched birds are likely to be poor producers in their first year.

Three years of research at The Game Conservancy, sponsored by Bibby's Sporting Feeds, indicates that pheasant hens produce

16

Be selective in your choice of stock.

eggs with higher hatchability and overall productivity when they weigh between 900 and 1100 grams in January. These birds are small to medium in size and weight and suit the current interest in the smaller bird for the shoot. However, selection on this basis does not automatically mean that they will produce good fliers for the next season – a lot depends on how the woods and crops are sited and managed, together with the post-release feeding regime. Selecting on the January weight basis will also mean greater efficiency in the hatchery and a more uniform chick. With regard to the cocks there is no detailed data but extremes should not be used; those around 1300-1400 grams are likely to be optimum.

Keepers may feel that they have little time to weigh birds, and will grade by hand and eye. But weights are worth the effort and easy to obtain when the birds are caught or penned in January. Large mechanical dial balances capable of taking 2–3kg with a sensitivity of 10–20g are suitable. Cheap electronic balances are now obtainable covering a similar range, but it pays to keep a standard known weight to check the functioning of the balance and a supply of fresh batteries. Since more birds will be discarded with this scheme, more will inevitably have to be obtained in the first place.

Some estates will want to produce a "type" of pheasant for the shoot rather than a varied hybrid of many strains. The cock can be chosen at this stage for nearness to ring-neck, black-neck etc. and any extremes of colour in the hens discarded. Most shoots will find that sticking to a single type results in easier and more productive rearing programmes. For example, a few melanistic chicks in a batch will often be attacked by their fellows, leading to increased aggression problems in the whole group. Melanistics should either be avoided or reared in fully separate batches.

Many shoots fear that inbreeding may be a long term problem but in practice, if you keep a stock of a hundred or more hens, this is very unlikely. If you have a good, productive stock which flies well it may be unwise to upset it by swopping cocks or buying in birds.

The choice of redleg is perhaps less exact. Now that release of hybrids between *A. rufa* and *A. chukar* has been prohibited, breeding stock must be examined for evidence of hybridisation. This can be detected most readily by examining the barred flank feathers. The pure redleg has no second black bar on these feathers. The degree of double barring will depend on the extent of hybridisation in the previous generation or generations.

Other features indicating a degree of chukar blood include a lack of black speckling on the breast and continuation of the black eyestripe forward over the bill. Chukars are also bigger than pure redlegs, so any very large birds are likely to be hybrids. This weight factor also has implications for sexing (see below).

18

Chukar hybrids have a double dark band on the flank feather. Note also the continuation of the dark eyestripe over the beak.

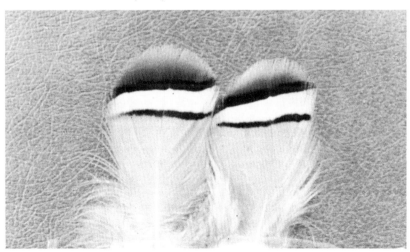

As noted in the scale of production section (see pp. 9–12), redlegs produce more eggs in their second and subsequent years. Keeping these birds does have disease implications, and while the risk of avian tuberculosis is low, it pays to bear it in mind. Birds which are kept off the ground are at a lower risk but even so any losses should be monitored for this disease. Being off the ground also reduces the risk of infestations by the parasitic worm, *Capillaria*, which causes wasting and death, and also of the occasional case of coccidiosis.

Redlegs hatched after mid July are very poor producers in their first year, but June and earlier hatched birds are much better. There are no data on suitable weights as we have for the pheasant, but any unusually small or large birds should be discarded. The dividing weight in February for cocks and hens lies at about 500–520g. An occasional cock will be less than this and a hen over this figure, but unless they are extremes they can be left in the flock. Other useful features in determining sex include the slightly stockier and more "bull-necked" appearance of the cock, and his "spurs". These latter are actually only small protuberances which occur in the same place as spurs on a pheasant. They also occur in hens, but not normally until over a year old, and so are a useful guide in first winter birds (see colour plates).

There is much merit in wing tagging all redlegs kept for breeding stock. Their sex and age can then be recorded. Also, successful pairs

Note the transverse white bands on this shoulder feather from a hen grey partridge (left). It is absent from the cock (right).

can be re-mated in subsequent years if they are overwintered in a flock with other birds. This is by no means essential, but it is likely to give improved production.

As with pheasants and redlegs, any grey partridge in poor health should be culled and any extreme of weight discarded. There is little difference in the average weights of the cock and hen, both being close to 400 grams. Sexing is therefore by plumage alone, and the key character is the barring and striping of the scapulars (shoulder feathers). These are diagnostic and are illustrated in the photo above. First year birds are better producers than older birds and hatches kept for stock should be taken from the early June period.

Obtaining stock

Breeding birds may be obtained in three main ways.

a) Catching up from the wild.
b) Home rearing and overwintering on site.
c) Buying in from external sources.

Each system has its merits and potential problems, and these can vary from species to species.

a) **Catching from the wild**

Catching from the wild really only applies to shoots which have a high proportion of hand-reared birds in their stock. Truly wild birds, and especially grey partridges, very rarely settle well to laying pens. Such birds are probably far better left in the wild and cared for there, where their full potential can be realised. Odd wild clutches which are dangerously sited, or which fall victim to agricultural operations, are best saved by using broody hens as foster mothers.

Any birds which are caught from the wild should be in pens before the end of the shooting season. There is no difference in law between taking a gamebird by shooting and by trapping even if the latter is for breeding stock.

i) *Types of catcher*

There are two basic types of catcher, one of which catches several birds at a time, and the other single birds. This latter type is now rarely used, but still has its value where populations are fairly low. It is especially useful for pheasants in outlying woods.

The individual bird catcher is suitable for the keeper who wants only a few birds for his laying pens. They are more like traps, in that when a trip-wire or stick has been touched, the catcher falls confining the single bird. No other bird can be caught in the catcher until it is emptied and reset. A broody coop or a "basket" made of hazel rods with a tripping device can be used, but because they can be tricky to set up it is suggested that the beginner asks a keeper friend for a practical demonstration. It is essential that they are checked regularly each day and emptied. At night they should be triggered and closed, or propped permanently open; this avoids the risk of a bird being caught in the evening and attacked by a predator.

Multiple catchers can be constructed in a number of ways. Lightweight catchers made of weldmesh or strong plastic netting, with or without a wooden frame, are very effective. A typical size would be 1m long by 0.7m wide and 0.5m high, with a tapering funnel

Single bird catchers are useful for outlying coverts.

Folding weldmesh catchers are easy to transport and very effective.

at one end. The main mesh should be about 8cm square. This size allows the birds to push their head and neck through, avoiding injury to the head. The funnel, however, is best made of 25mm chicken wire. It is normally about 0.25m in diameter at the outer end, tapering to 0.15m diameter over a length of 0.25m.

Catchers made of 25mm or smaller standard wire netting, whether with a swinging door or funnel entrance, are not so good because birds can easily damage themselves about the head in quite a short space of time. When constructing any catcher ensure that no cut wire ends are left facing inwards to injure a bird. Long spikes should be turned over and outwards.

ii) *Operation of pheasant catchers*

It is usual to set pheasant catchers where the birds are regularly fed. If food hoppers are temporarily left empty or hand feeding stop-

Place the bait in a band leading away from the entrance funnel where it can be easily seen.

ped, the birds will soon become hungry and enter a catcher to get at the bait, provided that it is clearly visible and not hidden in straw. In the weldmesh version this is laid in a 0.15m strip from the funnel to within 0.15m of the end of the trap and a little grain outside the catcher will guide the birds to the entrance funnel. Where the catcher is on a permanent or semi-permanent site, pre-baiting inside for a short time with the doors open or the funnels removed, or the catcher turned on its side, will help ensure good catches. Hoppers can be stood on top of weldmesh catchers when birds are previously conditioned to using them. They will then literally push their way into the catcher to get at the hopper.

The individual bird catcher is baited with a small quantity of grain at the back edge. If other foods are normally fed they should be used in preference to grain. When a catcher is set on an unestablished feeding site, three or four days of pre-baiting the area will probably be necessary, perhaps with the addition of a little straw.

Placing a hopper on top of a catcher is a good ploy where this is the standard feeding system.

Any catcher should be visited and emptied *regularly several times each day*. In particular a final inspection must be made just before the birds go to roost. Another choice is to open the catcher late in the day and reset early the following day. It is usual to set a catcher and then move to another ride or wood to set a second, returning to the first trap to remove the birds that are caught. On nearing a catcher care should be taken not to alarm the trapped birds – a sack or dark cloth quickly spread over the catcher will help quieten them before and as they are taken out. It is also helpful to arrange them so that you have a screened approach to avoid alarming the birds until the last minute. Should superficial injuries occur they can be treated with an aerosol spray containing a purple antiseptic, obtainable from a veterinary surgeon. Whenever not in use catcher doors should be tied back firmly, funnels taken out or stuffed solidly with a sack, or the release tripped.

Once caught, the birds can be transported back to the winter holding pens in standard wooden or plastic crates. Sacks are not acceptable, and are anyway illegal on public roads. According to the type of catcher, the number of birds available, the weather and the skill of the keeper, catching up the required number may take anything from a few days to a month.

The Christmas and New Year period is a good time to catch up pheasants. Working at this time allows any surplus cocks to be released for January "cock days", so that there is a balanced sex ratio left on the shoot for the breeding season.

Where reared birds have been tagged, it is possible to be selective, and release any untagged (and therefore probably wild) hens to breed naturally, while retaining birds of hand-reared origin for the laying pen. On the other hand it may be wise to retain a few wild cocks for the laying pen to help reduce any trend towards excessive domesticity in subsequent generations.

iii) *Catching up red-legged partridges*

The best time to catch up redlegs is near Christmas, since they tend to disperse earlier and more widely than pheasants, even if they are not regularly shot. They should ideally be caught up as soon as practical while still in coveys and using hoppers. Good management of

26

When birds have been tagged it is possible to select these for the laying pens and release any untagged ones to breed in the wild.

release pens for the reared red-legged partridge includes the provision of the same feeding and watering utensils, both inside and outside the pen as they have been used to while growing up on the rearing field. (This is naturally not always possible with bought-in poults.) When released they will continue to accept part of their diet from a hopper, thus providing a basis for catching up. Before the shooting season starts the release pen itself is removed together with the internal hopper and drinker, leaving the outside hopper as a regular feeding station. Later on when birds are needed for stock, this hopper is closed off and the ground baited around it. Multiple catchers are then placed alongside the hopper, baited with the same food and operated as for pheasants (pp. 24–25). Hoppers can also be placed on top of a suitably high catcher. Individual bird catchers are not worthwhile for partridges.

b) Home reared and overwintered stock

Home rearing and overwintering on site is an increasingly popular choice, but it does require extra resources compared to catching up from the wild. Most importantly extra ground will be needed to pen birds. This should not be the same ground as that used for rearing, or for laying pens, as otherwise there is a high risk of disease build up. There will be extra costs in terms of manpower and food, although the latter is partly balanced by the need to provide food for birds in the wild anyway.

The great advantage of keeping back a stock is the certainty about quality. There is no risk of invisible injury due to shooting, which might show only in reduced egg production. Also, all birds can be fed on a balanced diet which keeps them in good condition.

There is a question of genetic selection for domesticity in retaining a stock year on year. This could result in poor adaptation to the wild, and hence poor survival. On the other hand there is an argument which may have some merit, that catching up from the wild

Wintering pens need fresh ground to prevent disease building up.

means selection of the survivors of shooting. These are often the poor fliers which would not offer a testing target. If they in turn produce offspring which are likely to be poor fliers we could be selecting against good performance by catching up from the wild. Unfortunately, there is as yet no valid scientific research on these questions, so it is difficult to know what to do for the best.

The question of size of birds in relation to egg production has been touched on already. Suffice to say here that selecting a good sample of medium sized, uniform hen poults at six weeks is likely to produce a good breeding stock. The effect of hatch date on subsequent production has also been mentioned, but it is as well to repeat that for all three species early to mid season hatched birds are likely to be the best choice.

c) Buying in stock

Hatch date has particular relevance if you follow the third option and buy in breeding stock. In this case some kind of guarantee about hatch date is virtually essential otherwise there is a serious risk that you may purchase late-hatched birds which will be poor producers in the laying pen.

Where there is a shortage of space for overwintering or difficulty in catching up, buying in of breeding stock is another option. There is also the question of exchange of birds, usually cocks to "improve the blood". Whether there is any real risk of inbreeding if this is not done is far from clear at present.

Whatever happens, it must be borne in mind that any import of stock brings with it a risk of introducing viral and other diseases. If extra stock is needed, it should come from a known, well managed, healthy and disease free flock.

It should also be remembered that buying in stock is an expensive option. If you need to buy birds in order to produce enough, you may be well advised to consider buying the necessary day olds instead. In this way you can guarantee a fixed number of birds on a fixed date for the rearing programme.

CHAPTER THREE

Pens

Wintering Pens

The conventional'method of penning pheasants on grass during the winter in the same pen as for laying often results in the pen being stripped of vegetation leaving a muddy base unsatisfactory for both the bird and the egg. It is much better to winter the birds in some form of alternative pen to minimise this problem. Exactly what is done will depend on the weather, location, altitude, vegetation, soil, drainage and the manpower and equipment available. A few producers prefer to keep birds indoors, where questions of soil poaching do not arise. However, interruption of daylight length due to inadequate windows could lead to interruption of the breeding cycle, which is known to be photoperiod sensitive.

The most common choice of pen for both overwintered or caught up birds is made of ordinary rearing sections with a soft roof net over it. A temporary pen 12m × 15m (40′ × 50′) can hold 40 birds and will need two hoppers of 10kg capacity and two 10 litre (2 gallon) drinkers spaced around it. Larger groups in larger pens can cause problems both because of "mass releases" if weather damage occurs, and through any skittish birds being able to fly further and faster. This can lead to them colliding with side walls at high speed and result in injuries. The basic rule of thumb guide of 5 square metres per bird should be considered a minimum for the pen to avoid disease risk and poaching of the ground.

If natural cover in the form of bushes and shrubs is not available, it will pay to import some conifer tops or brashings to provide this, but avoid yew, which is poisonous. A dusting shelter will also be welcomed by the birds. This should be large enough to allow the birds to remain dry during spells of heavy rain.

Pheasants will normally be fed wheat on a regular basis and will take some grass or other vegetation if available. A pre-breeder manufactured pellet diet with a low energy content may have some small value on future performance but any winter diet should not

Provision of cover and shelter in the form of brashing helps to keep birds in good condition.

make the birds overfat. Pre-breeder pellets used in reasonable quantities will boost the uptake of vitamins and trace elements especially where there is a shortage of vegetation. Where birds are kept indoors a supply of pellets is more important and a periodic course of multi-vitamins and minerals can also be given in their drinking water.

Aggression between birds, especially cocks, can become a problem as the season progresses, coming earlier if the winter is mild and open. There are two ways of dealing with aggression between cocks. They can be penned separately from the hens during the winter in order for them to get to know each other and sort out a pecking order; once the laying flocks are set up the requisite number of cocks can be transferred. Alternatively the laying flocks of hens and cocks can be set up soon after catching up, before breeding behaviour starts to get under way in February. "Specs" can also be used in difficult situations to minimise attacks, but these *must* be the clip

31

on type and *not* those with pins penetrating the nasal septum; this latter type are illegal.

Redlegs can be overwintered on grass in flocks much as for the pheasants and there is no absolute need to separate out the cocks. However, recent trials at The Game Conservancy have shown that there is less trouble at pairing time if the sexes are kept separate. In February they should be sorted into their laying pens as developing aggression can be troublesome. Very often pairs are kept in their laying units throughout and apart from some possible initial aggression there is no problem unless a new partner has to be introduced. Flocks of birds can be kept indoors on shavings or in a large wire floored pen until required for the laying unit. For many years The Game Conservancy successfully kept two hundred birds, cocks and hens, in a raised series of five 3m × 3m interconnected pens with a further 3m × 3m covered section with perches, to go into during inclement weather. The pen was provided with five large drinkers and sufficient feeder space spread around the five units to take 50kg of food. This needed weekly refilling. Birds which do not have regular access to grass or other vegetation must be given a low energy pre-breeder diet to avoid deficiency disease, especially vitamin A deficiency, which occurs when wheat is the only available feed for long periods.

Grey partridges pose a special problem in that they can only be bred in pairs. If larger mixed sex groups are kept, serious problems with fighting will occur. The best answer to this is to sex them in autumn (see illustrations p. 20) and keep birds over winter in separate single sex coveys. These are then paired from late January onwards. Later pairings at the end of February or early March seem to result in less 'mis-matches', but mixed sex groups will not wait this long without fighting.

For small wintering groups, 3m × 1m A-frame pens are fine, but no more than half a dozen birds will be happy in such a pen. 3m square sectional pens with a soft roof net are adequate for up to a dozen birds, and large flocks can be kept in pens up to 12m square. This size is about the maximum for safety from injury. Feeding and watering is the same as for redlegs.

With both redlegs and greys in winter pens a dividing wall between the sexes is all that is needed. There is no need to have the separate sexes out of sight or sound of each other.

32

Grey partridges are best wintered in single sex groups.

Laying Pens

a) *Pheasants*

i) Siting and Construction

There are two main types of laying pen, fixed and movable. Siting of the pens is always important and they should be sheltered and have a southern aspect. The land should be light and well drained, with a surface that is reasonably smooth and level. Established grass and other herbage is ideal and will be appreciated by the birds. An open wood may sometimes make a suitable place for pheasant laying pens but there should be no lack of sun, grass or fresh green plant food throughout the season. *Ground where chickens, turkeys,*

33

To avoid stress try to ensure that the same worker, wearing the same clothes, attends to the birds' daily needs.

guinea fowl, ducks or geese have been running or where poultry manure has been spread must be avoided. Where possible, areas of ground should be used in rotation to avoid the build up of disease.

Precautions against foxes similar to those used to protect release pens (see Guide No. 10, Gamebird Releasing) are essential for larger flock aviaries, since twenty or so hen pheasants killed by a raiding fox could disrupt a whole restocking programme. These can include tall perimeter fencing (or garden wall), electric fencing and anti-fox fringing. Ideally the bottom of the wire netting should be dug in.

Occasional injuries may occur in any pen if the birds become frightened and dash themselves against the wire netting. All potential disturbance should therefore be discouraged, including stray dogs and cats which can be particularly troublesome. Visitors should be asked to keep at a distance, or to keep quietly on the move and not stand and stare. If possible, the same people should always tend the pens and it helps if they wear the same working clothes each day and go through a set routine of feeding, watering and egg collection. Stress is known to influence the quality of the shell.

34

ii) Small fixed pens

This system uses 3m × 1.5m pen sections, consisting of wire netting – 35mm mesh – nailed tight over a wooden frame, or plastic netting on a metal frame. The bottom 0.45–0.6m is boarded over or covered in plastic to give protection from wind and weather; the more sheltered the birds the better the egg production. Fixed pens on grass should allow the birds about 4.5/6m² each, which means that the usual group of one cock and six hens will need a minimum area of 30m², arranged as a 9m × 3m, or alternatively a 6m × 6m, pen. Soft netting over the pen helps avoid the need to brail, tape or clip the primary feathers of one wing of each bird. On the other hand, preventing the birds from flying in this way can reduce the chance of injury and therefore enhance egg production. Using netting can justify the slight extra cost by excluding egg and food scavengers such as crows, jackdaws and starlings. Egg production in small pens is generally better than in a large communal pen, although tending them is more time consuming.

Pens made with standard pen sections are a good system, since materials can be moved, cleaned and re-used for rearing later in the season.

Alternatively, small fixed laying pens may be constructed on twelve 2.5m larch poles driven 0.6m into the ground, carrying 2m high 50mm mesh wire netting. A board, sacking or corrugated iron screen is fixed round the bottom to give protection from the weather, with an anti-fox fringing for the top. This system is less economical because the 3m × 1.5m sections used in the former type of pen can be cleaned, disinfected and reassembled at the end of the laying period to make rearing pens.

Each pen should be furnished with low perches and a shelter of rough timber, about 1.2m × 0.75m and 0.6m high. Supported wigwams of evergreen branches, particularly western red cedar (*Thuja plicata*) or cypress – not yew – should preferably be placed in the centre of each pen to give the birds privacy and additional shelter, and encourage them to lay under cover in the same places. Coops are sometimes provided for the birds to lay in. Unless birds are encouraged in this way eggs will be more difficult to find and liable to quicker deterioration from the effects of frost, sun, rain or wind, and they will be more likely to be contaminated by harmful bacteria from soil and droppings if not found quickly.

The net can be held on at the top of the sections, with an overlap, by a variety of clips provided by manufacturers. Often the large C size plastic bit is used. To make it easier to move around in the pen, the net can be held up with a pole around 3m high with a cut plastic bottle on top to reduce wear on the net. (A full description of pen erection and roof netting is given in Guide No. 8, Gamebird Rearing.)

With roof netting over the pen considerable strain can be put on the sections in the event of strong winds or snow. This may cause pens to fall over or lift off the ground letting the birds out. Long runs of sections are also unstable. (See Guide No. 8.)

Larger sized fixed pens of the type discussed above can be built to contain more birds but in time the size of the net becomes prohibitive and many extra sections are needed.

iii) Communal pens

When a hundred or more hens, plus cocks, are being considered, a large communal pen comes into its own, and from the point of view of materials is the cheapest. On many estates old disused walled

A disused walled garden makes a good laying pen. Note the 'tent' of brashings in the foreground to provide nesting sites.

gardens have great potential as laying pens, especially since the walls make a valuable windbreak and reduce disturbance. This number of birds will produce good quantities of eggs in a communal pen of 900–1000m², although the pen can with advantage be larger. Much depends on how long the birds are to be penned, and the quality of the vegetation. Cover should be placed in rows down the middle, away from the perimeter where the ground can be beaten down by the constant passage of birds. A few bushes or small trees in the pen will be appreciated but they should not be too near the fence or wall or the birds may use them in an attempt to escape. With roof nets being impractical on such large pens, the birds will need to be wing clipped or brailed to prevent escape (see p. 43).

iv) Small movable pens

The standard movable pen for six hens and a cock measures 3m × 2m × 1.2m high, netted over. Compared with other systems it has the advantage that the birds can be placed directly in it after catching up and, because it is moved regularly, they always have clean ground and fresh vegetation during the laying period. These moves should be at weekly intervals, and when the weather is bad they may need moving more frequently to avoid poaching of the ground. Another advantage is that at the end of the egg production period pen sections and other equipment may be cleaned, disinfected and used elsewhere for rearing. Even small pens of this type will need to incorporate a shelter in the design.

(b) *Redlegs*

Redleg pairs, the sexes determined as described on p. 20, are normally accommodated in commercially available wire floored pair pens mounted on legs in batteries of five or six adjoining pens. In this system the problem of gapes is removed and liability to other

A small movable pen is suitable for a harem of one cock and six hens.

Wire floored pair pens help reduce disease problems with pairs of redlegs.

disease reduced compared to penning on grass. Injured or sick birds are easily spotted and removed. A lidded compartment at one end provides cover for the food hopper and water container or individual nipple system, while the opposite one provides a laying site with sand base. Problems arise if the hen lays her eggs on the wire netting floor, where they tend to get cracked. However, egg eating is more frequent in the box and, with cracking, up to 13% of the eggs may be effectively lost. Alternatively the pairs may be managed in a movable 3m × 1.5m pen or parallel "A" framed pens on grass. A few pairs can prove incompatible, with overly aggressive cocks bullying their hens. This usually occurs just after the birds are put together and is probably best solved by substituting a less aggressive (and younger) cock where possible.

Redlegs can be successfully flock mated in much the same way as pheasants. Note the wind shelter provided by the wall of bales outside the pen.

Flock mating on grass using a small communal system involves less initial outlay and daily labour in manpower but egg production will be a little lower. However, the higher rate of cracking in wire floored pens can often balance this. One cock to three hens is the usual sex ratio. The minimum size pen for 21 hens and seven cocks is 6m × 9m, but 6m × 12m is preferable. (Extra space may seem a good idea but can lead to serious problems in finding eggs as the grass and vegetation grows, whereas grazing by the birds keeps the grass in proportion in smaller pens.) The pure redleg is more excitable and prone to "stress" than the hybrid or chukar, and special care should be taken to disturb them as little as possible. If spooked into flight within a large pen, considerable damage can be incurred by birds as they hit pen sections at speed. Also flocks must not be over 40–50 birds in size.

One advantage of flock mating is that any birds which are surplus to pair mating requirements or cannot be sexed with certainty are not wasted. Such birds can be placed in the flock pen and have a chance to reproduce. Good cover, as described for pheasants, is very

40

important to minimise the effect of aggressive behaviour common in this species. Vertical hessian screens within larger pens can help to provide cover and wind shelter, and also reduce the risk of flying birds hitting the wire at speed. Wing clipping or brailing is an alternative solution to this problem. It is especially applicable to redlegs in that most people will retain their stock birds for several years, so there will be no need for release into the wild, where wing clipping would have implications in relation to subsequent flying.

c) *Grey partridges*

Grey partridges may only be kept in pairs. There are two types of pair pens. The traditional way is to use movable pens on grass consisting of units 3m × 1.5m × 1.3m high, with soft roof-nets, and provided with a shelter at one end. Alternatively pens made from aluminium tubing may be considered. The latter has the potential problem of being too light. This may be overcome by constructing the "A" frame ends out of heavier timber to help anchor the pen in the wind.

A pair of grey partridges in a small A-frame pen. Eggs laid in corners can be removed with minimal disturbance by lifting the side of the pen.

The disadvantage of being on grass is again the increased risk of disease and the consequent need for plenty of fresh clean ground. The alternative is a wire floored pen similar to that used for the redleg, but larger.

Preparing Birds for the Laying Pens

(a) *Sex ratio*

In flock pens pheasants are probably best mated in the ratio of one cock to seven hens. This allows for some loss of cocks before there is any loss of fertility, since ratios down to 1 : 10 have proved successful. For the flock mated redleg the ratio is higher, with one cock to every three to five hens proving successful.

One disadvantage of the small pen system with one cock and his harem is that very occasionally he may turn out to be a failure. This will not be discovered until the incubation is under way, when all the eggs from half a dozen or so hens will be found to be infertile. A sample of early eggs should therefore be candled (see p. 80) so that any impotent or infertile cock can be removed and replaced from spare stock. Pens will need to be numbered, and eggs marked on collection to detect this.

Extra birds will be needed to be kept in the groups to ensure that there are still enough cocks in the laying unit after any losses for whatever reason – hence the 1 : 7 ratio. It is usually not possible to safely introduce a new bird once the pecking order has been established. In a large communal pen, one cock will still try to assert his supremacy over the others, resulting in a certain amount of fighting but few losses providing there is plenty of space and cover. The "master" cock may also try to serve too many hens and fail, causing a slight drop in fertility. However, it is surprising how many hens a vigorous cock can cover. Wild cocks may also fly in over the top of an open pen and serve the hens. An occasional hen will be damaged by excessive treading but the routine daily watch should spot cases early on, when the hen can be removed to another pen to recover and continue laying without harassment.

Pairing partridges of either species is not always successful and

42

losses may occur. Late pairing from single sex groups keeps problems to a minimum. Once the birds are paired, move away from the pens and listen. By the sounds it is soon obvious which pairs are fighting and one of the birds can be exchanged. In time stable pairs will usually be established.

b) *Brails and wing clipping*

When pheasants are kept in flocks in large communal pens it can be impossible to provide a roof net large enough to cover the area. In these circumstances the birds will have to be grounded and prevented from flying out. This can be achieved either by fitting a brail or tape which holds one wing partly closed, or by clipping the primary feathers of one wing. In this way birds which attempt to fly are tipped off balance.

It is important to remember that the first fixing of the brail around the humerus (first wing bone) should not be too tight. It should be possible to insert a finger inside the brail. This allows free blood circulation to the rest of the wing. Ready made "ring brails" are also available. These are a little easier to fit single-handed, but have the disadvantage that there is no fixed tie around the humerus. Each time the bird tries to stretch its wing the brail tightens around the humerus – which could lead to long-term damage.

Special tape can be fitted in the same way, by tying off with a reef knot around the humerus (again taking care to leave space for circulation). The tape is then passed down between the first and second primaries, and tied back to the original loop.

Both tape and brails can cause some flight muscle wastage in the long term, and neither should be left in place too long. In normal circumstances an eight week maximum before swapping to the other wing is recommended. For laying birds this can be extended to twelve weeks, to allow a month before the first egg and two months of laying time.

The alternative of clipping the primaries of one wing is cheaper and easier but problems may arise when the birds are eventually released. The normal wing moult time for pheasants is in July, so wing clipped laying birds will rarely regain their power of flight until this time. Some keepers like to release ex-layers in late May or early

43

June, when they stand a chance of rearing a small late brood in the wild. Obviously wing clipped birds should not be released at this time since they would be very vulnerable to ground predators.

c) *De-spurring and saddles*

In the confines of a laying pen sexual activity is inevitably greater than in the wild – sheer proximity means that hens will be mated much more than in nature. The effect of this "over treading" is variable, but some loss of feathers on the back is virtually inevitable. In the most serious cases severe laceration of the back by scratching from cock birds' spurs, and even death, may result.

When such problems arise much of the trouble is likely to be due to overcrowding and lack of cover. Adherence to the guidelines given earlier on pen sizes and provision of brashings should minimise trouble, as well as helping to ensure low disease levels and good numbers of high quality eggs. Even so, it is probably wise to blunt the spurs of cocks used for breeding. The photographs opposite show how do to this using a bolt with a small hollow drilled into its head. This is fixed into a block of wood for stability and heated with a blow torch. Only the tip few millimetres of the spur should be burned off. Do not be tempted to use a debeaker to remove spur tips as this can cause serious injury and stress if you cut too far back.

Another possible solution to "over treading" now available is a special "saddle" to fit on to laying hens. These are reported to be great help but many would consider that the need to use them is a sign of severe overstocking and bad management!

d) *Spectacles*

Egg pecking or eating by pheasants in the laying pens can sometimes be a serious problem, and once it starts it is very difficult to cure. The old remedy of filling a few eggs with some noxious substance such as creosote or paraffin may have helped as a deterrent but it is probably now illegal under the Food and Environment Protection Act (1986).

44

A home made de-spurring device fashioned from a nail or bolt. It is heated using a blow torch and used to round off the end of the spur.

If egg pecking becomes a problem, plastic specs can be fitted.

One other possible cure is to fit "specs" to the birds (see illustration). These prevent the bird from seeing directly ahead, and so disrupt pecking without impairing feeding ability provided that the food is available in troughs or hoppers with a fairly wide feeding area. Narrow feed slots would be difficult for the birds to find.

Many keepers now routinely spec all pheasants before the start of the laying season, while others simply catch up and spec in those pens where egg eating starts. In either case, the need to use this remedy should be taken as the first indication of overstocking or shortage of cover in which to lay. It is also important to remember that the type of spec which is fitted with a pin which pierces the nasal septum is now illegal. The problem of egg eating seems in part to arise through an instinct of curiosity in young hens. It is normally a much less serious problem with second year birds. This has to be balanced against the increased disease risks inherent in using older birds for breeding stock.

Specs must be removed after the laying season whether the birds are to be released or retained for a subsequent season.

e) *Worming*

Any significant worm burden in laying birds can seriously reduce egg production. Birds which have been overwintered in pens on grass are particularly prone to having high levels of worms. For this reason many keepers now routinely de-worm their stock in early March prior to the egg laying season using mebendazole (Mebenvet) or fenbendazole (Wormex). These drugs are particularly valuable for gapes and the caecal worm *Heterakis*. Redlegs are prone to infestation with *Capillaria* when wintered on grass. They gradually lose weight, with odd emaciated birds dying over a long period during late winter, so that the keeper is not alerted to a problem. The preferred drug for this is levamisole. In all three species, nitroxynil (Gapex) is *not* suitable for laying birds, and should only be used for poults. If an outbreak of gapes does occur in the laying pen fenbendazole is the preferred treatment.

Management of Laying Pens

a) *Feeding and Watering*

The importance of providing laying stock with fresh high quality rations cannot be overemphasised and manufacturer's dates for consumption must be observed. If the birds have to put up with inferior or old, stale food, the production and hatchability of the eggs will suffer and the viability of the day olds may also be affected.

A good supply of fresh clean water is equally important as a bird dehydrated to any degree will lay fewer eggs – approximately three quarters of the weight of an egg is water!

In order to ensure that the hen pheasant has sufficient nutrients to build into the egg she should be gradually changed from the maintenance diet to a pheasant breeders pellet, with 18–20% protein, over a few days from mid to late February onwards. Partridges can be given the same pellets, although slightly higher protein levels in smaller pellets are available. Chicken layers pellets have an unsatisfactory nutrient make up. They are not suitable, nor are feeds for other species of poultry.

Some brands allow a little good quality wheat to be added – this will be stated on the bag. This amount is fixed and any excess will in effect dilute the nutrients available to the bird and may have a serious effect on egg quality.

The number of feeders must be sufficient to allow *each* bird easy access to food. Social competition between birds can result in some not having full access to food hoppers, leading to a reduced intake of food. One feeder might be adequate in a 9m × 3m pen but two would be better. In a large communal pen five to ten well spaced feeders should be provided for a hundred hens plus cocks. This overcomes the problem of dominant cocks "hogging" a hopper to the exclusion of other birds. A hopper must keep the contents dry and allow the food to pass into the feeding slot or trough without jamming. If the food is replenished weekly it will have little chance to deteriorate and become mouldy. But if the food does get damp or clogs it must be removed before fresh supplies are added.

Make sure that plenty of weatherproof feeders are provided for your birds.

A similar number of drinkers are necessary. They must be kept clean and always contain water. Ten litre galvanised drinkers are good and last well, but automatic watering systems are good too. The addition of a liquid vitamin supplement should not be necessary, but a dose once a fortnight costs comparatively little and may make up for any deficiency in the diet.

In general terms a pheasant consumes 60–90g of food per day during egg laying, or 450–700g per week. One hundred birds will eat 50–75kg per week. Partridges take a third to a half of this. Depending on the food, weather and rate of egg laying, a hundred pheasants will need three to five gallons of water per day and partridges *pro rata* as before.

b) *Grit*

In most places birds seem able to find enough insoluble grit to break down their food, but on soils lacking grit a small heap of clean coarse sand or fine gravel should be placed in the pen. Modern feeds pro-

A handful of mixed layers grit near the feeder is cheap to provide.

vide all the calcium that a bird needs to make shells, so limestone or shell grit should not be required. In spite of this, if it is felt that one of these soluble grits is needed place a little in the pen mixed with the insoluble type to avoid excessive intake of calcium. Mixed hen layer grit provides a good mix of calcium and insoluble grit and is ideal in this respect. Since it is so cheap, it is perhaps wise to provide it just in case there is a shortage.

CHAPTER FOUR

Egg Collection, Sanitisation and Storage

a) *Egg Collection*

Eggs should be collected at least twice a day, and preferably more frequently as labour and time allows; mid-afternoon and early evening are the best times to find most eggs. If an egg is left on the ground for as little as two hours it can be penetrated by contaminating bacteria and fungi. This can cause problems in the setter and hatcher in the form of "rots", "bangers" and dead embryos, as well as increasing the risk of disease. The general level of contamination in the hatchery will also be unnecessarily raised. Furthermore, an egg kept warmed by the hot sun will continue to adversely develop its minute embryo at this stage, causing subsequent degraded

Do not overfill buckets or baskets used to collect eggs, as you may risk cracking them.

growth and lower hatchability. Early in the season, evening eggs left out overnight may get unduly chilled or even frosted. Frequent collections during the day will also reduce losses in an unroofed pen from egg eating by predators. If, for any reason, only one collection is possible, the early evening one is most important.

Eggs can be collected in the plastic coated wire meshed baskets often used in egg washers. Alternatively a soft lined stiff sided bucket may also be used. Every care must be taken to avoid causing hair line cracks by gentle handling and not placing too many eggs in one basket or bucket. A small "egg net", similar to a child's fishing net, is handy for extracting individual eggs from difficult places without causing undue disturbance to the birds. This is easily made by attaching the foot section of an old nylon stocking to a small wire loop frame approximately 80mm in diameter and fitting it to the end of a garden cane. A deep plastic, spoon on a cane is another alternative and is ideal for partridge pairs' pens.

Communal pens have to be searched very carefully; particularly in a large one with long grass it may be difficult to be sure of clearing them every day. Groups of hens may well lay a "clutch" of eggs hidden under the grass with only a flattened strip of grass to suggest activity in the area. Many eggs will, of course, be laid in the open as well as under brushwood or other cover.

Slowly walking a systematically planned route, which checks each patch of cover in turn, reduces the risk of missing eggs. It also means that the birds will get used to a regular pattern of intrusion. This is likely to upset them less and result in better production. It is worth starting this a little before the laying season so that birds are used to the procedure when they begin producing eggs.

Similarly, with single harem pens, quietly walking the full perimeter so as to avoid panicking birds works well. Rows of pens with a gate at each end allow you to collect only to the middle, as you go up one side, removing the eggs from the other half on the return journey. This again reduces stress by allowing the birds to retreat quietly into the other half of the pen.

If it is intended to follow through the fate of the eggs, for instance to check if a particular pen is producing infertiles, they can be marked on the blunt end with a waterproof felt-tip. Different colours can indicate different days or pens. Such marking is best done at the point of collection to avoid any risk of muddles.

b) *Egg Sorting and Sanitisation*

Even an apparently clean egg can have disease or rot-forming organisms on its shell. Over the storage and incubation period they can penetrate the shell and cause serious problems. With the large numbers of eggs being handled nowadays, there is an increased risk of contamination and disease transmission. The constant need for producing first class chicks means that there is every reason to process only the best eggs and to reject those unlikely to hatch. In the longer term there will be fewer problems.

First of all, separate the visibly clean and dirty eggs into different containers and reject those unsuitable for hatching. Because eggs vary in size, shape, shell quality, thickness and porosity, no incubator can be set up which will cope efficiently with all the variations that may occur. In practise about 10% of the eggs collected from the laying pens will have to be discarded. Rough shells have a low porosity which allows little gas exchange and water loss, resulting in a dead embryo. At the other end of the scale an odd egg with a soft shell does occur. This is not a serious worry unless it becomes very frequent. Cracks let out too much water and the egg dries out. White patches do not present too much of a problem but to improve uniformity the worst should not be used. There is an association between successful hatchability and colour; blue eggs hatch at about half the rate of other colours and are best left out. The optimum egg is a mid to pale brown, while nearly white eggs and very dark brown eggs have a slightly lower successful hatching rate. Finally, there is the question of size. Extremes of size should not be used as the corresponding small and large chicks are unsuitable and may not survive so well. The best gamebird egg is of moderate size. For the pheasant this is around 34 grams fresh weight, the range being some 30–40g. The average redleg partridge egg is 21 grams and the grey partridge egg 15 grams. Again, any poor shelled partridge eggs should be discarded. With experience a reasonably uniform egg can be selected. Perhaps weigh a batch to get an idea of the weight range.

Sanitisation is very important whatever the supply of eggs. In some situations sanitisation must be done more than once. Contaminating bacteria and fungi are able to get inside an egg surprisingly quickly, especially if the egg is damp or wet. Hence cleaning should not be put off until later in the day, but should be carried out immediately after collection. The exact procedure will depend on the number of eggs and how dirty they are. Visibly "clean" eggs will still have some microbes on their surface. Eggs which are visibly clean can go straight into the sanitisation system, but the "dirty" category will normally need a little dry cleaning before washing.

Large lumps of dirt can neutralise the effect of sanitant and risk improper cleaning of the entire batch of eggs. If only a few grubby eggs are picked up during a collection they can be individually wiped with clean dry tissue and go straight for washing with the "clean" eggs. Occasionally in bad weather a whole batch of eggs will be muddy. They may need double washing to ensure proper sanitisation.

A typical system of dirt removal and sanitisation uses the "Roto-maid" washer. This is a heated bucket fitted with a thermostat which is gently rotated backwards and forwards a few inches in order to aid soil removal. The eggs are sorted into a plastic coated wire framed basket – often used to collect the eggs – which fits inside the washer. A fresh egg wash solution is ready prepared and heated

All eggs should be cleaned and sanitised as soon after collection as possible.

in the washer. There are a number of cleaning/sanitising agents on the market (see pp. 134–135), such as Ovation (High Foam) and Nusan II. Where the product is chlorine based it must provide at least 250 parts per million of available chlorine to be effective. When the thermostat indicates the appropriate temperature, at about 40°C, the temperature should be checked with a good quality thermometer. After ensuring the liquid is heated and well mixed the basket of eggs is placed in the solution for the correct time stated by the manufacturer, usually a few minutes, with the rotation mechanism turned on. When the time is up the basket of eggs is removed and allowed to drain. Shortly afterwards the eggs are placed in sanitised plastic storage trays. Each egg should be inspected on transfer and any that are still dirty will need hand cleaning in an appropriate warm solution. (**Note**: thoroughly wash hands in a hand sanitant before and after touching any eggs.)

It must be remembered that sanitisation is a chemical process. The active ingredient from the solution gets used up eventually. After this point the washing solution becomes a source of extra disease organisms, so making the situation worse. Solutions must therefore be fresh and *not* re-heated from a previous session. They must be used exactly as stated by the manufacturers. Products can lose effectiveness in storage, especially if the carton is not properly closed or is stored under damp conditions. Very often there is a "use by" date and this should be adhered to strictly.

Eggs can be cleaned manually having been placed in fresh solutions at the *proper* temperature and for the *correct time*, as specified by the sanitant manufacturers. Do not use a damp cloth to rub off the dirt as this may put more bacteria on the egg than it is intended to remove. This type of manual cleaning is less satisfactory than using a proper egg washing machine, but is helpful for the small scale producer.

For use on the really large scale, spray wash and bubbler machines are available which should use low foaming products. Some producers follow washing by use of an egg dip which is designed to reduce the risk of contamination in storage. Specialist fumigation cabinets are available for the larger producer (see notes on formaldehyde use in Chapter Ten).

c) *Storage*

The quality of egg storage is more important than most people realise. Although there is evidence that hatchability slightly increases during the first day after laying, the overall trend is downwards, accelerating after a certain time. Pheasant eggs lose a few per cent hatchability by seven days – the maximum age at which most eggs are set. This increases to around 10% by two weeks and much higher levels by three to four weeks. It is interesting to note that the hen can still produce good hatches from two week old eggs, indicating that we still have a lot to learn from her. If the eggs are stored well the loss of hatchability with time is minimal. With bad storage the loss rate is higher and soon becomes unacceptable. There are species differences and the redleg egg will, for example, store for much longer periods than that of the pheasant before significant losses occur. Badly stored eggs also decrease the viability of any chicks that hatch.

Since eggs normally need to be stored for a period of time before a useful setting may be made, the conditions of storage should be arranged to minimise loss of hatchability. A good store room is one that is cool and damp with steady temperatures. It should have little ventilation and be dark, rather than light with windows. A sheltered and insulated brick or stone building facing north is best, although a clean sanitised cellar is a good option. An insulated store room can often be designed and built cheaply within an existing building. A small cupboard-like structure with a volume of a few cubic metres will hold a surprisingly large number of trayed eggs on shelves.

The storage unit should if possible be kept *below* 16°C (60°F) and stabilised close to 13°C (55°F). Some gentle heating should be provided, preferably in the main building, if the store temperature would otherwise drop to near 10°C in the early morning at the start of the season. The control thermostat should be in the egg store. All surfaces should be non-absorbent, free of cracks and easy to clean and disinfect. The position of the store must be well away from potential contamination such as dirty eggs, hatcher waste and contaminated air from other rooms. Periodic fogging/fumigation may be of value (see p. 116ff.).

In very hot weather if the store temperature rises it can pay to place the trays of eggs singly on the clean sanitised floor. Here the air is often much cooler for the first few inches above the surface, especially if it is stone or concrete. The air should be very damp, about 75% or 80% RH, but not higher as there is a risk of the eggshell becoming wet and, if the temperature then drops, possibly introducing microbes into the egg via the shell pores. If the air is dry, it may be best to provide some source of extra moisture, even a humidifier, when storing really large numbers of eggs, but ensure that the machine is run hygienically so that bacteria do not develop and recontaminate the eggs. Some years ago accurately controlled stores on estates and game farms began to be used, and hatching success improved compared with the old situation.

Temperature is easy to measure. A good quality mercury "minimum and maximum" thermometer placed in the middle of where the eggs are kept is a worthwhile purchase for the store room, as well as other parts of the hatchery. Humidity is difficult and costly to measure accurately, but simple dial paper or hair hygrometers from gardening shops, laboratory suppliers or chemists are sufficient guides for the egg store.

Readily available plastic storage trays (see p. 74) are best, and being easy to sanitise are far more hygienic than the old papier mâché Keyes trays. Also they do not absorb fumigant making it ineffective. Sand trays and the like are to be avoided since they too increase the disease risk. Eggs may be stored ready prepared in the incubator trays if a spare set is kept. These should have plastic inserts and be sterilised before use (see p. 54).

Handling eggs at any stage should always be done with hands washed immediately before in a suitable hand sanitant (see p. 92). Hands should also be washed *after* the current and *before* the next job.

Theoretically, eggs could be set daily but this is impractical even for large scale farmers. Twice weekly is possible for the larger unit using walk-in machines, but generally eggs are set on a weekly basis with minimal loss of hatchability. They are stored large end up but modern information suggests tilting is not necessary over short periods. If, however, eggs have to be stored for longer than seven days, such as with early eggs, groups of trayed eggs should be tilted – using a carrier for large numbers – through 60°–90° once a day *from day one,* not day eight. This can be achieved by placing a block of wood alternately under opposite sides of the tray or carrier.

Redleg partridge eggs are interesting in that they can be stored for up to at least three weeks with surprisingly good hatching success. This is a valuable advantage, since egg production for this species builds up slowly and does not have the high plateau as for the pheasant. This means that reasonable numbers of eggs can be set from fewer hens. To achieve the best results eggs undergoing extended storage should be trayed small-end-up. They should be stored on a tilt to start with and the tilt reversed after a day or two, when they can be left flat, with the small end up. They must, however, be reversed back in the setter! In addition, the trays should be enclosed in thick plastic bags to minimise water and carbon dioxide loss from the stored egg. These techniques could also be applied to any long stored pheasant or grey partridge eggs. Mobile racks of trayed pheasant eggs in large units can be covered by a special large plastic bag – at least top and sides – with advantage, even over as little as a week, to reduce adverse water loss.

Purchased eggs (see p. 29) should always have been sanitised. They should be sanitised again on arrival, and also be rested for at least 24 hours before setting whatever their past history is *claimed* to be. Separate units for bought-in eggs should preferably be used at all stages of incubation and rearing, to minimise what amounts to a significant increase in the risk that disease might occur and spread to the rest of the operation.

CHAPTER FIVE

Basic Incubation Systems – The Choice of Methods

There are three basic incubation systems, each of which has its own particular merits. They are described briefly in the following pages, along with some discussion of their suitability for different requirements.

a) *Natural broody hen system*

Not so many years ago broody hens were used in large numbers to hatch gamebird eggs. Since it is labour intensive, and now there can be difficulties in finding sufficient reliable hens, the natural incubation system is far less popular. Modern views on disease control have also reduced its appeal. Even so it can be of particular interest to the very small unit. The broody hen has on the whole been relegated to minor roles, such as hatching out salvaged partridge nests, although they are still used quite widely for mallard or exotic species. A hen has the advantage that she is able to achieve a much higher rate of hatching than artificial methods and, even when the egg has had poor handling previously, she can still get a good hatch. Also, since she is a "chick rearing machine" too, she can carry out the full job of hatching and rearing with minimum outlay in equipment. The use of broodies is covered in some detail in Chapter Nine of this book.

b) *Artificial full-term system*

In this system a single batch of eggs run the full term of incubation and hatching. Most such machines are able to handle up to 300 eggs, with two or perhaps three batches being handled in a season in each machine. Typically, this type of incubator is run as a "still-

59

A couple of "still-air" incubators, such as this Gloucester, could easily produce sufficient birds for a small shoot.

air" machine with a single-layered egg tray. The term "still-air" is a misnomer since totally still-air would asphyxiate the embryo. The air is slowly moved over the eggs by convection, due to a temperature gradient across the machine generated by a heat source away from the eggs. This system is suitable for both the setting – up to 21 days – and hatching phases, with appropriate adjustment to humidity and ventilation. Eggs can be set monthly, allowing a few days for cleaning and refurbishing.

Other small machines use fan-assisted air flow for the setting phase but usually turn off the fan for hatching, when the thermostat will need adjustment.

The capital outlay for a full-term incubator is less than the larger cabinet machine (see next section). While several can be run at the same time there comes a point when a cabinet machine needs to be considered. A couple of "still-airs" will easily produce a few hundred chicks in a season for the small shoot, but suitable arrangements will have to be made for a supply of fresh eggs since each machine can only be filled once a month. This is an excessively long storage time for pheasant eggs in particular, so some sort of swap arrangement will need to be made with another shoot.

One of the disadvantages of the system is that eggs need regular turning to hatch well. In most "still-airs" this has to be done by hand several times each day.

c) *Artificial transfer system*

This system is suited to larger scale production from around 400 eggs per week upwards. It uses a larger cabinet machine as a setter to incubate the eggs for 21 days, before transfer to a separate hatcher. The normal system with such a machine is to fill one third of its capacity each week. Thus, once the machine is full with three batches, the space generated by transferring to the hatcher is taken up by a new batch of fresh eggs. The machine is thus run continuously throughout the season.

The system is much less labour intensive than the still-air system, with automatic egg turning normally incorporated. It also avoids the risk of possible contamination of the machine from the mess and debris of hatching, and is thus more hygienic. The capital outlay is high, but the cost per egg set decreases with increased numbers.

Incubation Requirements and Hatchery Design

During the incubation phase eggs must be kept at a steady temperature and humidity for much of the process. This special set of environmental conditions is produced and maintained by the incu-

A modern cabinet incubator for use with a separate hatcher.

bator. However, wide fluctuations in the environment outside the machine can have a significant effect on its efficient running, and result in poor hatches or weak chicks.

The hatchery building needs to be chosen or constructed with the special environment of the incubating eggs in mind. Very often the hatchery is set up on an unsatisfactory *ad hoc* basis, even when large numbers of eggs are involved, in order to save costs. It is far better to design and build a separate hatchery or, if this cannot be done, to carefully modify an existing structure along certain lines.

In essence eggs should be taken in at one end of the hatchery and the chicks and their debris out at the other. All surfaces should be easy to clean and sanitise regularly, and the temperatures and air-flows should be kept as close as possible to desired levels. Humidity is generally not easy to control except in the egg store, but should be kept stable when possible. A washing-up area attached near to the hatcher room and washing facilities near or in the egg-cleaning room should be provided.

Since hatcheries can be different in size, handling from an odd hundred or so eggs in a season to tens of thousands per week, layout is highly varied. A possible, though generalised, layout based on the essential requirements given in the previous paragraph is shown in Figure 2. If this type of layout cannot be considered, for example

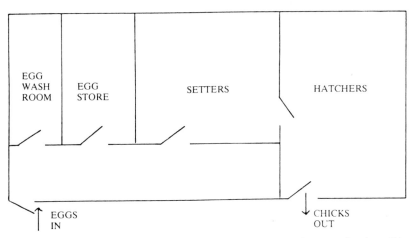

Figure 2. Layout for a hatchery to minimise the spread of contamination. (Not to scale.)

63

because only one room is available and dividing walls would be impractical, the layout should nevertheless be systematic such that each stage follows on from the last, minimising cross contamination. Every effort should be made to make the system as controlled and hygienic as possible in order to improve hatches and to avoid the spread of disease.

Whether a building is adapted or a special hatchery is built, there are a number of points which must be kept in mind.

A north facing situation and shade will lessen temperature changes. A smooth, slightly sloping, concrete apron around the base together with appropriate drainage helps to reduce the amount of soil getting into the building. The building itself should have insulated walls – a galvanised shed is not suitable as the temperature will fluctuate too much. There should be no windows which catch the sun. Existing ones will need shutters to exclude all direct light. It can pay to paint the outer surface white to reduce heating effects. There should be a liberal supply of hot and cold water to both wash-up areas and adequate drainage to the exterior. A separate mains electric supply will have to be laid on. A proper trip should be fitted by a competent electrician. A battery operated alarm system in both the hatchery and keeper's house will warn of mains or equipment failure. Very often earth safety trip circuits are fitted to the mains and these can operate unexpectedly even though there is no failure on the public mains.

The various rooms can be specifically built or created by putting in dividing walls and false ceilings. All surfaces should be painted in gloss or washable emulsion to aid high standards of cleanliness and hygiene. The floor should be smooth, painted and slightly sloped towards an opening to an external drain. However, incubators and hatchers should be carefully levelled when they are installed. Since there will be a lot of water used on the floor, walls should be completely sealed at their contact with the floor to keep out wet and stop microbial growth in the crack. Enough space to work in must be arranged – remember that setter and hatcher doors have to be opened fully to handle the trays. The ceilings need to be at least 0.5m above the highest point on the equipment, with about 1m spacing around each piece of machinery to allow easy access and room for the air to move without forming stagnant pockets.

Good sport requires attention to detail at all stages of production.

Sexing of grey partridges is easy and reliable using shoulder feathers. Hen (left) has transverse bars but these are absent from the cock.

Cock redlegs (above left) have a larger head and neck than hens (above right). Note also the knobs on the back of the legs on cocks (below) compared to hens.

Eggs should be stored in a cool damp place.

Date marking trays in the incubator ensures that there is no confusion over expected hatch dates.

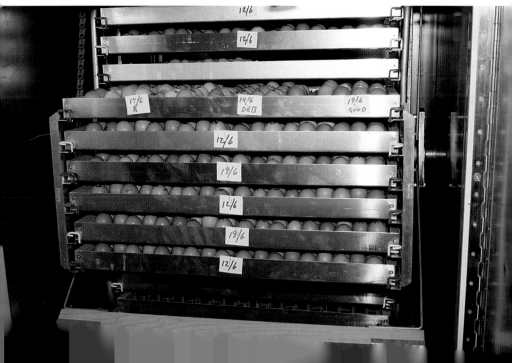

A properly constructed incubator house gives much better results than an old shed.

Expert examination of failed eggs can give important clues on any incubation defects.

Fresh air is taken in on a low level through baffled vents and extracted on the opposite side at a high point with a fan. Some eight changes of air per hour in the setter room and four per hour in the hatcher room are needed. The air flow can be controlled by altering the fan speed or by fitting a shallow box over the exit port with a sliding door which can be fully open or if necessary closed right down. It is important to control this in combination with the temperature in the rooms as this can influence the temperature in the machines, especially still-air machines. It will obviously save a lot of adjustment if the room temperature is stabilised. In a small set up a simple plug-in (13amp) thermostat and 1kw panel heater may be all that is needed. The setter room should be kept at some point between 15°C and 20°C and the hatcher room close to 20°C. More than this and the air flow through still-air hatchers may be reduced, causing an undue build up of carbon dioxide. The egg store should not go above 16°C and preferably should be kept at 13°C. The egg wash room should be kept cool so that the eggs cool down quickly to below 21°C when collected or once they are washed.

At times, such as when transferring the eggs from the setter to a hatcher, it may be necessary to raise the temperature temporarily by altering the room thermostat and reducing ventilation.

Humidity is crucial in the egg store and this should be around 75–80%RH. It is also useful to have a high humidity in the hatcher room especially when the vents are closed down to their minimum to raise the humidity within the hatcher to the highest possible level. Slowing the room ventilation a little, wetting the floor and raising the temperature a few degrees will all help. Once the hatch is complete and the chicks are drying off the ventilation can be increased to the maximum rate. (This is explained in greater detail on page 88.)

Hatching inevitably produces a lot of debris which will contain microbes, some of which may cause disease. Proper facilities for disposal of waste, unhatched eggs, etc. will be needed to minimise the risk of cross contamination with other batches. There will be a need for a properly designed wash area where hatching equipment can be cleaned and sterilised. It may be advantageous to have separate exits for hatch waste and hatched chicks, again reducing the risk of cross contamination from any diseased eggs which have failed to hatch.

Types of Incubators and Hatchers

Within the two basic systems of artificial incubation mentioned on pages 59–61, there are a wide range of different types of incubators of varying characteristics and capacities. These can be divided into the following five categories.

a) *Small desk-top types*

These machines handle anything from a dozen to a hundred pheasant eggs. They can be based on either the still-air or forced draught principle, and some may include automatic turning. It is inevitable with such small capacities that control of the environment within the incubator is somewhat limited, except in very expensive specialist machines used by keepers of rare or expensive exotic birds. As a consequence hatch rates are not likely to be consistent.

They are nevertheless popular with those who wish to produce small batches at home, and can be particularly valuable for saving hot clutches where the hen has been killed on the nest. Nevertheless, small scale producers would be wise to consider whether broodies provide a better alternative.

b) *Still-air full term machines*

These machines, typified by the old Ironclad, Gloucester and Glevum, and the modern Bristol and Brinsea, can have capacities of up to around 300 eggs. They are usually free standing, can be run on various fuels (ie paraffin, propane gas or electricity) and often rely on hand turning. Many of these are used simply as hatchers for eggs incubated in larger forced air machines.

If eggs are to be set in weekly batches then, in common with desk-top types, four machines will be needed. Incubators of either of these types can also be rather difficult to clean, so the risk of cross contamination between batches may be high.

c) *Forced air full term incubators*

This type is typified by the Hamer, in which the air is driven by a fan. There are least two sizes available, taking either 500 or 1000

66

eggs per week. Eggs must be turned by a hand-operated lever and are transferred on the 21st day to separate hatching trays in the top of the machine.

d) *Small cabinet forced air setter*

These are typified by the Marcon and Western machines. They are called setters because the eggs are only kept in them for the 21 day 'setting' period. They are then transferred to some kind of hatcher since the environment of the forced air machine is not suitable for hatching gamebirds. Capacities start at around 750 eggs (ie 250 per week) and rise to a weekly intake of 10 000.

All incorporate automatic turning, and therefore require the eggs to be packed into the trays since these are tilted in the turning process. The air is kept in continuous movement by paddles driven by an external electric motor when the machine is in operation.

e) *Walk-in setters*

For the very large producer, walk-in machines are available from a number of manufacturers, including Western and Buckeye.

f) *Hatchers*

As noted in (b) above, most hatchers are basically still-air incubators in which the correct environment for hatching gamebirds can be created. Some recent models do use a modified fan system for air flow. They vary in size from the small still-airs of 75 pheasant egg capacity up to large walk-in machines to be used in conjunction with walk-in setters. They are only used for the five day hatching period, and can thus be cleaned and refilled on a weekly basis. As well as the old types listed in section (b), modern makes include those by Bristol, Marcon and Western.

g) *Cost of incubators*

The capital cost of large incubators is high, but on a per egg capacity basis it falls as the size increases. Also running cost per egg drops as size increases, since the environment within the incubator is more easily maintained. The larger cabinet machines, with their automatic turning, require less frequent attention on a day-to-day basis compared with those that need manual turning. All this makes a single large machine a more economically viable proposition than a number of small ones, especially since hatch rates are also likely to improve.

For those intending to purchase a new incubator, there is considerable wisdom in buying something with a little spare capacity. This will allow expansion in the future, without imposing enormous extra capital or running costs.

CHAPTER SIX

The Requirements of Eggs During Incubation

In nature the parent bird provides a suitable environment for the development of the embryo. This involves keeping the eggs at a fairly constant temperature of about 37.6°C. The hen normally goes off the egg each day for a short while to feed, and the outside naturally cools a little at this time. However, fluctuation at the centre of the egg, where the embryo is developing, is much less. If the bird were to leave for too long, chilling of the embryo would slow development, and in extreme cases lead to death. At the other end of the scale, if egg temperature rises development is accelerated. If the temperature becomes too high, it kills the embryo. As the chick grows, it produces more of its own body heat and towards the end of incubation it can thus sustain a longer period with the hen off the egg.

Humidity is important to the incubating egg. In too dry an atmosphere eggs lose too much moisture, and this can lead to small, weak chicks or the death of the embryo through dehydration. Excessive humidity produces over-large chicks which have insufficent room for hatching and usually die in the attempt.

The hen also turns the eggs many times each day. This is very important to the physiology and proper development of the chick and the various membranes attached to it within the egg. These are distinct from the membranes attached to the inner calcareous part of the shell. Without turning, the embryo, along with its yolk, tends to float to the top of the egg and is then unable to grow correctly.

The normal time of incubation varies in length from one bird species to another. The times for the main species with which we are concerned in this book are as follows:

Japanese quail	17 days
Grey partridge	24 days
Redleg partridge	23 days
Pheasant	24 days
Mallard	28 days
Greylag goose	32 days

Artificial incubation attempts to offer the same conditions as those provided by a sitting hen in the wild.

70

In common with all animals the developing embryo needs oxygen for respiration. For birds in the early phase of incubation this is obtained through the porous egg shell, by blood vessels in close contact with the inner membranes. At the same time, carbon dioxide produced by respiration passes out, along with some water vapour, thus increasing the air space within the egg.

During the last few days of incubation, the now almost fully developed chick changes to air breathing with its lungs. This happens by the chick breaking into the airspace with air exchange going on through the shell in this area. This stage is known as internal pipping, to distinguish it from the external pipping (chipping) which occurs as the first phase of hatching. This is when the chick first breaks through the shell, and can be followed by as much as 36 hours of apparent inactivity, without the beak tip showing. Chicks can often be heard calling to each other during this period, and there is evidence that this is involved in synchronisation of the hatch. In certain weather conditions, and especially during thunderstorms, the hatch may be delayed.

Artificial incubation machines are designed to emulate the conditions described in the last few pages. They must be thoroughly reliable, particularly in relation to temperature. Variations of as little as a fraction of a degree can have a significant effect on hatch rate and chick viability.

CHAPTER SEVEN

Incubation using Transfer Systems

The system used for the overwhelming majority of gamebird eggs, and also the basic technique used by The Game Conservancy's trials unit is incubation using transfer systems.

Preparing Cabinet Machines

Machines should be cleaned and sanitised (see p. 116ff.) prior to being periodically run for a day or two each month during the winter to help keep them functioning properly. This also helps to reduce the risk of damage by damp conditions. Any final running-up should never be left until the last moment since faults may still be found which could be difficult to repair. It pays to arrange for the equipment to be serviced during the winter. A few crucial spares should, however, be obtained and kept in hand against emergencies. These include a mercury thermostat or thermistor unit, wicks for the wet-bulb thermometer, drive belt spares, capsules, fuses and electronic plug-in controls, together with a supply of *distilled* water. A stand-by generator in case of mains failure should also be considered.

Time is needed for a machine to settle down to its correct working condition. *Two days* before the first setting switch on the serviced incubator and check the working values. The temperature will always "hunt" up and down a little but this variation should be no more than a fraction of a degree; nor should the temperature go over 37.8°C. Any abnormal running should be investigated and corrected but leave the machine for several hours before deciding if it is running correctly. The mercury thermometer type of thermostat cannot be adjusted and would need replacing in most cases. Sometimes the column of mercury breaks if it is badly shaken, inadvertently raising the working temperature. Check with the manufacturers whether it can be rejoined without altering the accuracy. Cooling in a deep-freeze or with solid carbon dioxide may be helpful. If in doubt, put in a new one. Check the alarm system. This is controlled by two ether-filled capsules, usually mounted on

72

the front of the incubator or immediately behind the control box. These are a safety cut-out, in case of an overheating failure of the main controls.

The humidity should be raised to give a wet-bulb reading of about 28–29°C to check the system, but it is emphasised that this may need to be altered later during incubation. The wick must be fresh, clean and white and the bottle filled with distilled water. Any sign of solids or yellowness indicates it must be replaced with a new wick. The turning mechanism must be checked for correct functioning. Once the machine is running properly, fumigate or fog it to remove any residual and unwanted surface microbial contamination (see p. 116ff.), then leave it ready for use.

The hatchers should be serviced at the same time as the setter, checking that they operate correctly. The heating wires or panels, for instance, sometimes fail and stay cold, and must be replaced. The final run-up need not be done until about Day 18, when the working conditions can be set and verified. Give the machine several hours to settle down at its correct level and check the alarm system.

The smaller sizes of hatchers, up to 1000 eggs, are designed to be operated on a bench or table, not on the floor. A careful check of levelling and stability of both setters and hatchers is important at this stage. This should be carried out with a spirit level. Any departure from a proper level could result in the improper filling of water trays with consequent humidity problems.

Setting

The cabinet setter is used for the first 21 days with turning and moderate humidity. (Note that redlegs are set for 20 days.) Eggs should not be set the same day as they are collected, since there is evidence that hatchability is slightly higher after a day. It is also preferable to move them out of the cool store overnight into the setter room to allow them to warm up a little before setting. This reduces heat-shock to the minute embryo and lessens the risk of a film of condensation forming on the shell as the trayed eggs are put into the setter. This film could aid bacteria getting into the pores. Also, all operators should wash their hands in a suitable sanitant before and after handling any eggs or machines.

Nowadays, most traying is carried out using plastic inserts provided with the tray. Older type trays can have inserts fitted after removing any dividing strips. The eggs are trayed vertically, big end upwards. This is far easier than the old system of traying the eggs touching each other with the consequent need for paper "wedges" to hold the whole thing together. Since eggs are not in direct contact, it also reduces the chance of cross contamination from any infected ones.

Pheasant inserts are available in two sizes, the white type for standard eggs, and a black type for those a little larger than average. Partridge eggs have their own appropriately sized inserts. These may be too small for some of the larger redleg eggs, in which case they can safely be set in standard pheasant inserts.

Egg grading has been mentioned in the egg collection and storage section, but it is as well to keep an eye out for any cull eggs which were missed earlier during the traying process. Hairline cracks which were missed at the collection stage may be more obvious by now.

Plastic inserts make traying eggs much easier than it used to be.

Keeping a spare set of incubator trays allows eggs to be trayed and stored from collection, reducing the workload on transfer days.

Cracks are emphasised by water or sanitant which has penetrated during storage.

With eggs being set weekly, a third of the positions for the trays are filled at the start of week one, a third at week two and a third at week three. When the first batch has been in three weeks it is transferred to the hatcher and replaced by the fourth batch. The second is replaced by the fifth and so on. When the last three batches as planned are in the machine each in turn is transferred after 21 days until the setter is empty.

In order to help achieve a steady air-flow over the eggs, and an even temperature, the trays are spaced through the carrier in a special sequence rather than putting them together. This also has the advantage that the loading is better balanced so that mechanical vibrations are not set up to shake or jerk the eggs or wear out the equipment.

Setter Temperature

Since the air in a cabinet machine is circulated by paddles or a fan it becomes well mixed and the egg temperature will be close to that of the air around it. These machines may run at slightly differing temperatures within the range of 37.5°C to 37.7°C. Heating is electrical, the temperature being controlled by means of a sensitive thermostat.

Over the years thermostats have developed from the low sensitivity double ether-bellows operating a levered switch, with its inherent relatively large response to the weather's high and low pressure systems that pass over, to single temperature mercury contact thermostats. In more recent years thermistor type sensors and electronic controls, which are often adjustable, are used, although an ether-bellows is frequently used for the back-up and warning system.

Each system has its problems. As already mentioned, capsule control fluctuates with the weather systems. Also the ether capsules need changing as metal fatigue eventually causes cracks and a loss of ether which makes them inoperative. A functional cold capsule will have obvious liquid in it when shaken. Capsule controlled temperatures should be run at an average value rather than repeatedly adjusting the thermostat in an attempt to stabilise the temperature further, as there is often a considerable time-lag in the system and the extremes in temperature may well be adversely increased. In normal circumstances with this type of control the temperature will be graduated in degrees and will fluctuate between 99° and 100°F.

Mercury contact thermostats are essentially sensitive, accurate thermometers with wire contacts inserted to make contact with the column of mercury above the bulb. As the temperature increases the mercury expands up the capillary stem to make contact with the second wire, turning off the heat via an electrical relay. They are reliable devices but a severe jolt, such as when a door is slammed, will break the mercury column and cause the temperature to increase beyond what is needed. This will be detected on the external reading thermometer commonly found on cabinet machines and the safety back up. The break in the column is usually very narrow and a hand lens is often needed to detect it. It is better to have a replacement handy rather than attempt to rejoin the mercury at the time.

Either ask the manufacturer at a later date how to do this or return it for servicing. It is surprising how easily the volume of the thin glass bulb can be changed, thus upsetting the thermostat's accuracy. In the meantime, the machine can be safely run on the back-up with the temperatures adjusted accordingly.

Modern electronic controls are reliable but should anything go wrong there could be problems, as the circuitry is complex and needs an electronics expert to repair it. Many makes now have replacement plug-in control units (relay) to overcome this problem.

Turning

In practice, turning should be frequent throughout the setting period. Most machines automatically turn the eggs through 90° every hour which provides optimum hatchability without undue wear on the machinery. The trays of eggs are carried in a pivoted frame or drum which is tilted gently backwards and forwards very slowly, without vibration or jerks. Some machines tilt stacks of trays rather than drums. A mid-position switch is provided so that the turning can be stopped with the trays level, in order that the eggs may be inspected or the trays changed.

A resettable turning-counter shows how often turning has occurred since the previous inspection, giving a warning that all is not well if the number is low. Many machines are fitted with a hand turning lever for use in the event of a breakdown (refer to manufacturer's instructions). Hourly turning is not essential in the circumstances, turning three or five times per day until repair is effected should be adequate. The drum is normally fixed on a centre shaft locked on to the turning mechanism by grub-screws. These have been known to become loose, the turning mechanism operating without tilting the drum, causing a very poor hatch. The counter had, however, shown the correct number of turns!

Humidity and Air-space

Another very important factor is the development of the air-space in the egg by the continual loss of water through the egg-shell's pores during incubation. Research by The Game Conservancy shows that most hatched pheasant eggs lose about 14% of their weight during the first 21 days of incubating (Figure 3).

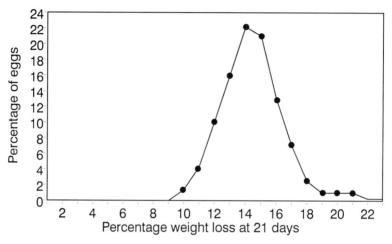

Figure 3. Weight loss at 21 days – hatched eggs.

Cabinet and walk-in machines are fitted with a variety of systems to control humidity. These may be in the form of water trays, drip feeds or heated water trays within the cabinet. Some very large machines may have an air supply that is fed into the machine at a certain temperature and humidity in order to achieve the desired internal conditions.

The air in the setter must not be saturated 100% relative humidity (%RH) with water (anything more would come out as mist or fog) or else the egg will not lose water. In practice, machines are run at about 50% humidity, ie the air has 50% of the water it could hold if it were saturated at the given temperature, in this case 37.6°C. With this degree of dampness the average egg will lose the desired 14% weight to leave the correct size of air-space.

The humidity within the setter can be physically measured in a number of ways. The least accurate and cheapest method, giving a rough guide, is the paper hygrometer which can be bought from horticulture shops and meteorological equipment suppliers. A little better and costlier is the hair hygrometer, but the usual way is to use the wet bulb thermometer technique which is usually supplied with the setter. This is based on the cooling effect due to the evaporation of water by less than saturated air (the wet finger technique to determine wind direction).

Cabinet machines using this last method have an extra thermometer, which has the mercury bulb covered in a special absorbent cloth wick suspended in a bottle of sterile distilled water, free from dissolved solids, fitted inside the compartment. As the air at 37.6°C is driven past the wet wick cools the thermometer bulb to a lower temperature. Providing the air speed is above a certain value the thermometer reaches constant temperature, in this case 83°F or 28.3°C "wet-bulb", indicating 50% RH; 82°F would indicate 48%RH, 84°F 53%RH. Hence a lower wet-bulb temperature means drier air and a higher one damper air. Thus we have a means of knowing the humidity of the air and to what extent it may have changed. Eggs vary in porosity for a variety of reasons including their tendency to become increasingly porous as the season progresses, and they consequently need damper air to compensate. The wet-bulb temperature therefore needs to be gradually raised. Humidity is something that the keeper or hatchery manager can learn to control for himself by altering the water regime to suit local conditions. In time it will be possible to fine-tune the system so that the number of changes are minimal.

Sometimes the local environmental conditions are so damp and warm that no extra water is needed. Indeed in some cases water vapour has had to be removed from a hatchery's air in order to keep the setter humidity down. This happens in the West Country but in the dry, cooler eastern part of the country water is often needed throughout the incubation period. Water is normally supplied, if needed, by filling a water tray which is provided with the machine. If the humidity becomes too high, but some water is still needed, a piece of sterilised expanded polystyrene will cut the surface area of the water, and hence reduce evaporation. Tap water sterilised with a suitable product is better than rainwater and offers less risk of contamination.

By the end of the setting phase it is the egg that shows whether the conditions have been right. There are two ways in which this may be checked: (i) by candling, which is also used to check fertility and development, and (ii) by weighing.

(i) *Candling*.

Candling an egg in a darkened room by shining a powerful light through it produces much useful information that can be used to develop hatchery techniques and improve hatches. Besides providing air-space information, candling can also be used to check "fertility", the presence of dead embryos or bad eggs. The importance of water loss has already been discussed and candling is the most common method used to follow the development of the air-space during setting.

There are a number of candling devices on the market but the most useful for estates is the small cylindrical type (see below) which can be moved around on the top of the egg to illuminate the air-space without having to remove it from the tray. Weekly checks, carried out in a darkened room, of a representative sample of about

Candling a sample of eggs allows the progress of incubation to be checked.

thirty eggs, will quickly show whether *on average* the air-space is the proper size. If it is not, action can be taken to adjust the air-space by alteration of the water regime or to a lesser degree by changing the ventilation. In time it will be possible to tell how much water a particular machine is likely to need each day under typical conditions; but be prepared to alter the amount if there is any marked change in air-space development. The approximate size of the air-space in an egg is shown below for the three common gamebird species at weekly intervals (Figure 4).

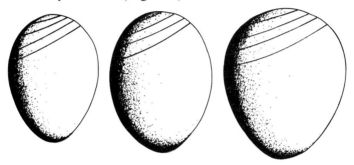

Figure 4. The air space, at weekly intervals, for grey partridge eggs, redleg partridge eggs and pheasant eggs (from left to right).

As an alternative a simple wooden candling box can be made at home for more general or occasional use, but the light must be powerful enough (c.100w) to penetrate heavily pigmented shells such as pheasants. There should be a 30mm hole in the top surrounded by a ring of cleanable plastic against which the egg can be placed, so as to cut off all the light except that which passes through the shell. If the egg, held by the narrow end, is placed up to the hole and rotated, the full extent of the air-space will be seen. The disadvantage of this is that the eggs have to be handled individually, making it a slow procedure. Also there is a risk of contamination of the shell by bacteria from the fingers – hands should always be washed both before and after handling eggs.

As well as air space development, candling also shows much about embryo development. If candling shows no real opacity other than a slight yellowing due to the yolk, the egg is said to be "clear". In some instances they will be infertile. A proportion will be fertile but any cloudiness on the yolk due to an early stage embryo can

81

only be found by breaking open the egg. It is worth noting that an infertile egg when broken open generally keeps its yolk intact and the white clear as in a fresh eating egg. Fertility becomes obvious at around seven days when definite opacities will be seen, along with reddish blood vessels lining the shell.

As development proceeds the whole egg, apart from the air-space, becomes opaque by 21 days. It then pays to discard clears and bad eggs with fluid contents. When candling is carried out to find and mark reject eggs, not only will there be better spacing and more room between the eggs in the hatcher trays, but unnecessary contamination will also be avoided. At any stage during the setting period eggs that smell or are seen to be oozing liquid should be removed at once to prevent the spread of infection by bacteria and fungi. The eggs should be removed carefully in case one explodes – a "banger" – to make matters worse. One advantage of the plastic inserts is that a banger or contaminated egg can be better removed without disturbing the other eggs. Should plastic inserts not be in use, replacement eggs will keep the other trayed eggs in place, but these will in effect be sacrificed for the sake of the stability within the tray.

(ii) *Weighing Eggs*

This is a rather more accurate way of determining whether or not the air-space is developing correctly but provides no information on other development. While weighing can be carried out on individual eggs using small sensitive electronic balances, many eggs still need to be weighed to allow for the considerable individual variation that occurs in a batch. It is easier to weigh trays of eggs to determine the average loss.

By 21 days a pheasant egg should lose about 13–14% of its initial weight. Fortunately the rate of weight loss is steady and estimates can be made early on, say at seven days, of the likely 21 day loss. Water can then be added or removed from the setter as required. For example, at the 14% level 5000g of trayed eggs should lose 700g by 21 days (20 days for a redleg) or 230g each week. A 10% loss and 16% loss would be 166g and 270g respectively each week. Other weights are in proportion. A balance capable of weighing up to 8kg to allow for the weight of both eggs and tray with a sensitivity of

Don't forget to allow for the weight of the tray when measuring moisture loss by weighing.

83

10g or 20g is needed to make full use of the method. Mechanical or spring balances of this sensitivity are available and not too expensive. Some form of special carrier may be needed to take the tray. *Do not forget to allow for the weight of the tray in making your calculations!* Also always ensure that you mark the tray(s) which are being monitored, so that the same eggs are weighed each time, the first weighing taking place immediately before first loading into the setter.

Ventilation

Eggs consume oxygen during incubation. They also give out toxic carbon dioxide and lose water. Hence ventilation is needed to keep the correct levels of these gases in the air around them. This is normally achieved with adjustable vent holes in the top and bottom of the machine (see manufacturer's instructions).

There are a number of general points to remember which will help in coping with the widely differing conditions that are possible. Since a cabinet machine is normally operated as a multi-stage setter, during the early and late parts of the season it will contain relatively few eggs, many of which will be at an early stage of development. Hence the requirement for oxygen replenishment and removal of carbon dioxide is low and the vents only need to be opened a little. But from about the middle of the second week onwards, carbon dioxide production greatly increases. For this reason the manufacturers often suggest that the vents are opened wider once part of the incubation period has elapsed. This is particularly important when there are young as well as mature embryos in the incubator, because the former are more sensitive to the carbon dioxide that is being produced in quantity by the older ones. Without ventilation, lethal levels could build up; however, excessive ventilation could affect water loss, particularly during periods of low humidity.

Preparation of Hatchers

After 21 days in the setter (20 days for redlegs) the eggs will be transferred to a hatcher (with the exception of the Hamer, which has

84

its own built-in arrangements). These are available in a great variety of types and sizes. They should be pre-cleaned and switched on well before they are needed and then fumigated or fogged. Allow the temperature to settle and check that this is at the same level as for incubation. If not, final adjustments can be made as required. 24 hours prior to transfer the water trays should be filled to capacity (so as to ensure enough water to last through the entire hatching phase of up to six days). This allows sufficient time for the water to warm to hatching temperature. Take care to position the water trays correctly, as this can have a critical effect on air flow through the cabinet. This is controlled via adjustable ventilation ports in the back of most hatchers. Water sanitant can be added with advantage.

After 21 days the eggs are transferred from the cabinet incubator to a special hatcher.

Transfer to still-airs and hatching

When the eggs have been incubated for 21 days they are transferred to the still-air hatcher. At this stage, if all has gone well, none of the eggs should have pipped. If any have, it is likely that the temperature in the setter has been too high. Before transfer the eggs should be candled and cull eggs removed (see p. 80) to save space and prevent needless contamination in the hatcher. This is best done in a temporarily warmed room.

The eggs are placed on their sides in the hatching tray, making sure that none are trapped with the pointed end upwards. The tray should not be over filled. As a guide it should be three quarters full with eggs spread throughout, giving chicks room to hatch. *No further turning is carried out.* A wire cover is placed over the eggs to keep the hatched chicks on the tray. If the tray is not full a smaller cover should be used to restrict them to part of the area.

For about two days the eggs are allowed to so-called "dry down" by reducing humidity. This is achieved by fully opening the vents. During this time the chicks will be breaking through into the air-space, a process known as "internal pipping". The chick is changing over from respiration via the blood vessels on the inner surface of the porous shell to lung respiration, initially breathing the air in the air-space. This is replenished through the pores in the shell, which under very damp conditions tend to be smaller. Drying-down under less humid conditions opens them a little and allows a better exchange of carbon dioxide and oxygen until external pipping has occurred and the chick is able to breathe directly the air passing through the hatcher.

In a good hatch where everything is proceeding according to plan, once about a quarter of the eggs are pipped it is assumed that all the embryos that are likely to hatch are through into the air-space and have established lung respiration. Pipping, to make the first hole to the outside world, starts the exit from the shell, and hatching now goes on apace. This quarter pipped stage usually occurs about 48 hours after transfer and the humidity must now be raised to prevent the shell membranes from becoming dry and tough and the chick losing too much water. A good plan is to check on this by opening the door and quickly examining one tray for signs of chipping. An accurate count is not needed, and you should bear in mind

Hatcher trays should have a mesh cover to prevent chicks escaping.

that some eggs will be pipped on the underside. Do not turn or disturb the eggs. In a modern machine, the portholes are now closed down to a smaller aperture, thus reducing the air flow and raising the humidity. Closure varies according to local conditions but must not be complete or the chicks will die of carbon dioxide poisoning. Hatcher humidity can also be raised by increasing the room temperature and wetting the floor.

From now until the hatch is virtually over, *do not be tempted to open the doors just to see what is going on, because this will adversely affect the membranes and make it harder for the chick to get out.* Also taken care not to knock or jolt the machine or bang nearby doors, as this can all have an adverse effect on the hatching chicks.

On Day 24, if the temperature has been correct throughout the incubation, most of the chicks should have hatched. With the hatch

Hatched chicks can be transferred to special boxes in which they may be transported without food or water for up to 24 hours.

now complete, open the portholes completely to allow the chicks to dry off and rest. Extra ventilation of the hatcher room will help speed drying. By the 25th day the chicks should be dried and on their feet. They should be removed from the hatcher before losing too much water and becoming deyhdrated. Any hatch will be spread over a period of time; a few chicks will be early, most near a mid-point of time and some late. A decision has to be made when to take off the hatch so that the maximum number of good quality chicks is taken. The earliest are ignored as they will be too dry and the few late ones cannot be allowed to hold up the bulk of the chicks.

A really good hatch comes off crisply and indicates quality eggs and good hatchery methods. Conversely, a dragged out hatch implies poor eggs and methods.

Planning output

The necessary equipment ultimately depends on the number of poults to be reared and released. Working back from this, assuming for the present purposes average results, 125 six-week poults can be expected from 200 eggs. Thus a typical cabinet setter taking 1000 eggs per week would lead to about 625 poults per week requiring, say, three 220 chick brooder units or the equivalent each week. If six weekly batches are set, total production would be 3750 poults for release. Over a ten week period around 6000 poults would be produced allowing for a small gradual decline in production as the season progresses. Cabinet machines range from 400 eggs per week upward into the tens of thousands.

The number of matching still-air and other type of hatchers that are required will depend on their type and size, but one large one or up to three smaller ones should easily cope with the output from 1000 eggs per week. When dealing with a much larger number of eggs the choice of setters and hatchers lies between a single large unit or several smaller ones. The former, though more costly in terms of total capital outlay, results in a lower cost per egg.

Many estates find it convenient to set and transfer on Fridays, and hatch Monday/Tuesday. This leaves Wednesday and Thursday to clean, fumigate and fog the hatchers and run them up ready for the next transfer on the following Friday. The timing of the whole operation involving, for example, six batches would be as follows:

BATCH	SET	TRANSFER	HATCH
	FRIDAY	FRIDAY	MON/TUES
1	Day 0	Day 21	Day 24/25
2	Day 7	Day 28	Day 31/32
3	Day 14	Day 35	Day 38/39
4	Day 21	Day 42	Day 45/46
5	Day 28	Day 49	Day 56/57
6	Day 35	Day 56	Day 65/66

Note: Redlegs would be set on the Saturday so that they hatch on the same day as the pheasants.

CHAPTER EIGHT

Incubation Using Full-term Machines

The commonest alternative to using a cabinet setter and separate hatchers is probably the use of full-term "still-air" machines. The term "still-air" is slightly incorrect, in that air movement still occurs. This is by convection rather than some form of mechanical movement as in the "forced draught" machines.

Planning

Two or possibly three batches of eggs, with a four week interval between settings, can be put through a still-air machine in a season. Because the eggs should be no more than one week old, it may not be easy to collect sufficient fresh eggs from a stock of birds without holding a relatively large number of excess hens for a long period, which uses a lot of feed and wastes many eggs. Two or more machines will largely overcome or eliminate this problem. Bought-in eggs or those from wild birds provide alternatives; in addition some keepers exchange eggs to fit in with each other's incubation programme. However, it must be remembered that the risk of spreading salmonellosis and other diseases is greatly increased by such swaps and the eggs, which must be from healthy stock, should in any case be properly cleaned, sanitised and fumigated whatever the source. The capacity of still-air incubators ranges from about 20 to 300 pheasant eggs.

The Hamer type (See p. 95ff.) is rather different, in that it is designed to take three separate weekly batches in much the same way as as cabinet setter. These are then transferred to a built-in hatching compartment after 21 days.

Running up

Much of what has been said for the preparation and use of the still-air hatcher applies, with some modifications, to these full-term incubators (see p. 86ff.). They should be cleaned, sanitised and fumigated or fogged. They can then be run up to the correct temperature and humidity with moderate ventilation.

Incubation with full term still-air machines

These incubators can run on three different fuels, electricity, bottled gas or paraffin. If either gas or paraffin is being used, it is important to remember that this consumes oxygen and produces carbon dioxide, so more ventilation will be needed. Also, a cooler room than normal for forced air machines will help air flow by convection across the eggs, but this may not apply to small desk-top incubators (such as the Curfew and Polyhatch). The Glevum, Gloucester and Ironclad, particularly in the case of gas or paraffin models, will require a 48 hour start up period to achieve a steady temperature. They run best with a small flame.

Control of temperature within these machines is by an ether capsule located in the centre of the roof. This adjusts a chimney cover via a 6″ needle and weighted balance arm, thus increasing or decreasing the temperature within the cabinet. These machines are normally operated at a nominal 39.7°C (103.5°F) with a special mercury thermometer suspended 50mm above the egg tray floor. This apparently high temperature is dictated by the temperature gradient across the eggs, and results in a normal level of 37.6°C at the centre of the eggs. When this temperature is achieved the chimney cover should have a clearance of approximately 3mm. This can be corrected by the central brass adjustment screw. It may also be necessary to move the counterbalance weight to suit the individual capsule. With a paraffin burner, always use good quality fuel and wicks, and avoid adjustment to the flame once this is set up. Temperature control in electrical models is usually basically the same, except that the capsule controls a microswitch connected to the heater element.

In the early part of the season it may be difficult to achieve a high enough temperature. To counteract this the normal procedure is to fit a layer of felt underneath the chick tray to reduce air flow. As the eggs develop and begin to produce their own heat this is removed to increase available oxygen. Control of airflow by adjustable portholes may be available in some machines (eg Bristol and Ironclad).

During the setting phase internal water trays are filled and operated according to the manufacturer's instructions with fresh tepid tap water that has previously been boiled. But it may be necessary to adjust the regime to suit the eggs in use and the local environment. Where there is an external humidifier, as in a Glevum or Gloucester machine, fill it with warm previously boiled fresh tap or distilled water. Many old machines have long since lost their water trays, in which case extra humidity can be provided by lightly spraying with *tepid* water after turning (see pp. 78–79 for guidance on how to determine whether this is necessary).

Hand turning of eggs is essential for the first 21 days. They should be rotated horizontally through 180° backwards and forwards at least three and preferably five times each day. The reason for the odd number of times is so that they do not always spend the longer night period laying the same side, as this could affect development. A simple method to assist the accuracy of turning is to mark each egg on one side with a felt-tip. On alternate turns the marks should be visible.

Hands should always be clean and *sanitised when handling eggs.*

Where trays are not full, the eggs should be kept towards the centre. Temperature can vary across the tray, so it is wise to reverse it each time the eggs are turned. Always close the door whilst the tray is out for the eggs to be turned. Hands must always be clean and washed in hand sanitant before touching eggs.

Some incubators have an external lever or turning device which avoids the need for opening and individual handling of eggs. It is nevertheless wise to mark the eggs and check perodically to see that this is working properly.

Hatching with full term still-air machines

Turning ceases after the 21st day when the eggs should be candled and any clears and part-formed embryos can be removed to allow extra space for hatching.

The details of producing a good hatch depend on the machine, but the basic procedure is described in relation to hatches with cabinet machines. One point of design is, however, pertinent. Some early still-air incubators have a lower tray into which the hatched chicks can fall, having been attracted to thè front edge of the egg tray by light coming through a small window. They then complete their drying in the lower tray. In this type there is a small section to be removed from the front of the egg tray on the 22nd day to allow this to happen.

On the 22nd day the temperature may rise by a degree or so as the chicks begin to "work" towards hatching. This is not a cause for alarm. Late on the 22nd day (21st day for redlegs), visually examine the eggs for signs of chipping, without unduly disturbing the eggs. If things have progressed normally the quarter pipped stage (see p. 86) should have been reached. If chipping has not started it could indicate too low a temperature (so check incubator before using for another batch). Meanwhile, close the incubator and wait for twelve hours before checking again. Once the quarter pipped stage is reached, humidity needs to be raised. This is achieved by increasing room temperature, wetting the floor and filling any water trays or closing ports as appropriate to the particular machine. If no water trays are available, a wad of cotton wool or a clean towel soaked in sanitised tepid water should be rolled up and placed on

93

the front of the trays. This should not cover or touch the eggs. A good indication of adequate humidity is condensation around the inside edges of the observation window. It is difficult to achieve too high a humidity.

Once this is complete, leave well alone until the chicks are hatched on the 24th day.

Summary of schedule of operations. A summary of general instructions for full-term models may be useful, especially as those for older machines are not readily available.

ELAPSED TIME	*OPERATION*
Day 0	Set eggs during afternoon after bringing eggs to room temperature overnight
Day 1	Begin turning programme and continue until the start of Day 21. Early morning, mid-morning, afternoon, late afternoon and evening at least for hand turning.
Day 7	Check development of air-spaces of a few eggs. Adjust portholes if necessary. Remove one felt.
Day 14	Check air-space as before. Adjust conditions. Reject any bad or early dead embryo eggs.
Day 21	Finish turning eggs. Ensure that they lie flat or with big end slightly tilted up. Turn off fan in machines fitted with one or modify air flow according to manufacturer's instructions. Start to "dry-down" eggs.
Day 22/ Day 23	When a quarter of the eggs have pipped, raise humidity considerably, eg by partially closing ports, filling inner trays with warm water or placing wet cotton wool in egg tray. When a door has to be opened, carry out any operation as rapidly as possible and shut it. Then leave well alone but check the

temperature. Again in old machines do not be tempted to open the incubator unless it is *certain* that the water has dried out and needs replenishing.

Day 24/
Day 25
If the temperature has been correct throughout setting, most of the chicks will have hatched. When the hatch appears complete open portholes, remove extra sources of water. Box chicks.

Because there will inevitably be variations in the hatching period, it may be possible to box some batches on Day 24; yet others may not be ready until Day 26. Late hatches mean that the machine is running at a low temperature, or the eggs are of poor quality from having been stored too long under the wrong conditions (see p. 129ff.). High temperatures lead to very early and long, staggered hatches.

Incubation And Hatching With Forced Air Full Term Machines

The typical example of a forced air, full-term incubator is the Hamer, but there are many smaller desk top examples. These latter are in many senses similar to the full-term still-air machine in that they are filled with a single batch of eggs and run through to hatching before cleaning and refilling. In common with forced air cabinet setters, the Hamer is designed for weekly batches of eggs, but has its own built in hatching section at the top.

Initial Preparation

In common with other incubators the Hamer must be set up level and also with space for access to the side door. Temperature is controlled by ether capsules located in the back of the machine above the fan and heater elements. Beneath the fan are two ventilation points, one permanently open and the other adjustable. Power supply to the heater is controlled by a double and treble capsule bellows unit similar to that found on still-air machines (see p. 76). The capsules operate a needle which parts the two electrodes, thus

95

The Hamer has its own hatching trays in the top.

96

cutting off the power. These are located under the two covers on the top of the machine at the back, with adjustment via screws. *These terminals are live and carry the full 240 volt supply.*

Adjustments can be made by an insulated knob. The electrodes should be filed flat (with the mains off) at the start of the season, and periodically checked for carbon deposits due to arcing. Between the two electrode covers there is an neon bulb which acts as an indicator for the heaters. When the bulb is on, the heater elements are supplied with current. In front of the bulb is an on/off switch for the fan. This should be switched off about 30 seconds before operating the door, to allow the fan to stop running. Failure to observe this time lag will result in much cool air being drawn into the machine and a consequent loss of humidity.

In common with other incubators the machine should be switched on 48 hours before introducing the first eggs. Final adjustments can then be made to the temperature settings. The machine is normally run on the treble capsule, with the double acting as a safety back-up. To set the bellows, once the machine is up to approximately 100°F (it is normally fitted with Fahrenheit thermometers) turn the left hand (treble capsule) control knob until the light comes on, and the temperature reaches 100.5 to 101°F. Now turn the right hand control (double bellows) half a turn clockwise. This sets it to 101°F so that it will cut the power supply if the treble capsule fails to operate correctly. Now cut the adjustment back on the treble capsule so that the light goes out at 100°F. At this stage the thermometer should continue to hunt up to about 100.5°F and then fall to close to 99°F before the light switches back on. This is the normal working range of the machine.

Loading the Machine

Inside the Hamer P21 there are nine setting trays, three hatching trays and two water trays. One of the latter is located at the bottom and is used to control setter humidity as required. The other is directly under the hatching trays.

The setting trays take 170 pheasant eggs. These are placed in rows on their side between the wire dividers directly onto the corrugated floor. Do not fill the front or rear spaces, as eggs in these rows are

97

liable to crack during turning. Do not overfill the rows; ten pheasant eggs across each row is the normal amount. To turn the eggs (which should be done three or five times each day) gently pull the handle towards you while holding the tray in with your thumbs. The base of the tray will travel towards you, thus turning the eggs. For the next turn the handles are pushed back. Once each day slide the trays out and check that the eggs are still equally spaced and laying level on their sides. Before adjusting the position of any eggs ensure that your hands are cleaned and sanitised.

Humidity

The Hamer is run with humidity control as in other forced air machines.

Hatching

The Hamer has its own hatching trays at the top, but some users prefer to transfer to a still-air hatcher (see p. 86ff.). In either case the eggs should be candled on the 21st day (see p. 80). To hatch in the Hamer, the eggs are transferred to the hatching trays, and the water tray beneath this filled. Sometimes there is a little difficulty in obtaining a high enough humidity. It can be increased by temporarily limiting airflow through the top vents by placing a table tennis ball on them.

When turning the younger eggs in the setting part, do not forget to allow plenty of time for the fan to stop running before opening the doors as this helps to conserve humidity for the hatching eggs.

If for any reason you need to inspect the hatching trays, and when removing the hatched chicks, always pull out the bottom tray first. The tray above acts as a roof, and you risk injuries to chicks if you pull this out.

Once the hatch is off, both water trays and the hatching trays are removed, cleaned and disinfected. The bottom water tray is then returned and refilled to provide humidity for the eggs in the setting phase.

98

CHAPTER NINE

Incubation and Rearing with Broody Hens

The incubation of gamebird eggs and their rearing using hens or bantams is as near to the natural method as artificial rearing can get. The system produces a top rate poult, which is often said to be quicker to adapt to the rigours of the outside world than its brooder house reared cousin. Broody hens have been used for rearing ever since the artificial rearing of game began. Within each individual broody exists the natural equivalents of all our modern day rearing technology – the incubator, the brooder house and the stimulant to the chick's instinctive behaviour. The advent of intensive rearing techniques led to the rapid loss of much of the age-old knowledge on the broody hen system. However, The Game Conservancy is today receiving an increasing number of enquiries from its members and from small shoots with part-time gamekeepers as to how they might economically rear a small number of hardy, good quality poults. The small time game rearer cannot afford or easily justify the costs incurred in the purchase of incubators and artificial rearing equipment. With time available, the enthusiasm, and the desire to rear a small number of birds, the broody hen may well provide the best option.

The hand rearing of gamebirds was initially achieved with broody hens in coops – a method which became known as the 'open field system' because of the absence of runs. The rearer had to be in constant attendance during daylight hours and feeding had to be done several times in a day. The high demand on labour makes this system uneconomical today, particularly for a small number of birds. Another factor against the open field system today is the difficulty of obtaining a sufficient number of broody hens or bantams to sit all at the same time.

An alternative system that is used at The Game Conservancy and found to be a viable proposition for the small shoot is the use of broody hens with movable pens. This method of game rearing has given very good results for many years, and the percentage of chicks successfully reared to the poult stage can often be well over 90%.

Incubation and rearing with bantams can produce top quality poults, but is only practical on a small scale.

The advantages of this system over the open field are numerous and almost certainly outweigh the few disadvantages. Birds grow quickly and evenly; diseases can be isolated at once; losses from feathered predators are nil, and should be negligible from those on the ground. Rats sometimes squeeze in under the pens and weasels can get in through mole runs, but this is rare. A further advantage of this system is that there are no losses from young birds straying away from the coops and scavengers such as starlings and rooks cannot steal the chicks' food – and coincidentally spread disease. Finally, compared with the open rearing field, a much smaller acreage is needed for movable pens.

However, this system is more labour intensive per bird than the use of brooder houses or intensive indoor systems, and will prove uneconomic for the full-time professional keeper wishing to rear a large number of birds. But for the amateur or part-timer with only a few dozen or perhaps a couple of hundred to rear, it does have advantages over the modern day alternatives. Firstly, it usually produces excellent quality, well-feathered poults. The capital outlay on equipment is far less than the cost of brooder houses, pens and heaters, and it is an ideal method by which to rescue the eggs from the odd badly sited wild nest, or those found during hay or silage mowing. Such eggs can be collected and successfully incubated under a broody, even though they may appear to be cold when discovered. No cracked or damaged eggs should be used. The good eggs should be candled the following day to give some indication of the previous incubation period in the wild and thus the approximate hatching date.

Equipment Required to Rear 250 Birds

2 sets of 7 sitting boxes
12m of 100mm × 25mm sawn board and 12 wooden pegs
14 broody hen sticks and tethers
1 small hand shovel
1/4 bale good quality hay
1 small tin louse powder
Dummy eggs (or hard boiled bantam eggs)
12 coops (with shutters)

101

24 pen ends
12 3m × 1.5m plain pen sections
12 3m × 1.5m gated pen sections
12 4pt red and white plastic drinkers
12 small feed dishes (150mm plastic plant pot saucers)
12 small hanging hoppers (home made)

The Setting-up of the Sitting Boxes

Choose a quiet sheltered site, preferably along the north side of a wall or shed so as to provide the sitting boxes with shade during the hottest part of the day. First remove turf from the site to form an oblong cutting, 0.6m × 6m along the wall. A level surround should next be created used the sawn board and pegs. This is then filled with well trodden soil (see Figure 5). The grass up to a metre in front of the boxes should be tightly mown at least one month prior to the start of incubation, and weekly thereafter so as to create small lawn. The sitting boxes should be set on top of the soil approximately ten days before the actual start of incubation. (The raising above ground level helps prevent the base of the nests from filling up with water during heavy rain.)

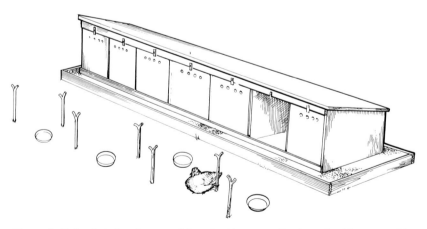

Figure 5. Raised sitting boxes with tethering pegs. Designed with removable fronts.

Sitting boxes were traditionally made in blocks of seven, the seventh box containing a hen kept primarily as a spare in case one of the others should fail in her duties. The spare bird's chicks are used to make up full broods by replacing infertile eggs amongst the clutches of the other hens, thus using the hens and equipment to their fullest. These seven hen blocks may possibly be difficult to obtain today. Ideally they are manufactured from 9 or 12mm exterior plywood, giving insulation and weather protection for the sitting hen. Holes should be made for good ventilation. There are several door designs: lift up lids, lift out fronts (the design preferred by The Game Conservancy) and hinged fronts. No flooring is required.

Once placed on top of the raised soil base, shallow nests are formed in the base of the boxes using moist soil which has been passed through a 9mm sieve. It is important to shape the nest properly. If it is too deep or bowl-shaped, the hen will have difficulty in turning the eggs in the centre; ideally it should be saucer-shaped so the eggs can gently roll towards the centre. The soil is topped with a 25mm layer of hay which has been chopped into 50mm lengths, so preventing entanglement around the hen's feet and legs and thus possible damage to the nest or eggs when lifting her out for feeding.

The Choice and Preparation of the Broody Hen

The best of all broodies for gamebirds are old fashioned farmyard hens, which can be hard to come by these days. Those from battery cages should be avoided. All hens or bantams used for incubation or rearing should be fully feathered. Birds from deep litter houses can be used, but their feather condition should be checked beforehand. In the absence of a good farmyard supply, an alternative source is the modern free range egg producer.

For pheasant rearing, the best hens are Rhode Island, Light Sussex and Moran types, all being of medium body weight and well feathered, It is not economical to use small bantams for rearing pheasants. Such small birds can only rear ten poults – a waste of the broody hen equipment.

For rearing redlegged or grey partridges, the bantam is the bird to use. If broody hens are used, particularly for grey partridges, severe losses can occur through the extra weight of the hen accidentally crushing the chicks as she moves around within the coop. Some of the very small bantam breeds, especially the hard feathered varieties, should also be avoided as they tend to be highly strung in nature and, due to their small body frames, they are difficult to keep in the coops. The best type of bantam for partridge rearing is the Silkie cross. This is a cross between the pure Light Sussex bantam and a pure Silkie cockerel. This produces an excellent sized bantam which usually has a good temperament. Pure Silkie bantams should be avoided for grey partridge rearing wherever possible. The hairy texture of the feathers can sometimes cause high losses due to the grey partridge chicks becoming entangled and subsequently choked to death. The average sized bantam should comfortably cover 20–22 partridge eggs, thus maximising efficient use of the bantam and equipment.

The normal practice is to purchase broodies on approval, as some will not accept being moved from their chosen sites and will go off being broody. After a few days these birds are returned. If producing home-reared broodies, do not rush the birds' move from their chosen site to the sitting boxes. From the moment of becoming broody, they should be allowed to remain sitting for a few days before the move. This allows the rearer time to handle the birds, thus getting them accustomed to human contact. The usual way of checking for broodiness is to slide one hand under the front of the bird's breast with fingers upwards and lightly fondle her breast which should be warm and bare. If broody, she will respond by tucking in her wings and raising her hackles, while emitting a low clucking sound.

If broodies have to be transported any great distance, this is best done in separate crates with a base covering of hay or straw. These should be well ventilated but covered to reduce the light. If transported collectively in a single crate, broodies will usually fight, resulting in some of them losing their broodiness.

All broodies should have their legs inspected before purchase for signs of 'scaley leg'. This is caused by a parasitic mite which lives under the scales. The symptoms are distorted scales and a thickening of the legs, which themselves are dry and flaky. Any bird seen with this complaint should be rejected as the infestation can be passed

on to the chicks. Should it be seen in one's own flock, an old fashioned cure is to immerse the legs up to the feather line in domestic
paraffin. Alternatively, seek veterinary advice for the necessary
treatment.

Any birds showing a heavy infestation of lice, with their under-
feathers becoming matted together, particularly on the neck and
head, should be rejected, along with other birds which appear off-
colour. All broodies should be de-loused prior to being put into
the sitting boxes, however clean they may appear to be. Poultry
louse powder is usually available through local agricultural merchants. The powder is easily applied by holding the broody by both
legs in one hand with her head down. A small amount is sprinkled
into the base of the tail and vent area, and down each side of her
breast. The powder is then gently fluffed into the feathers.

To introduce the broody to her new sitting box, gently place her
on the ground in front of the open box so that she is able to see
a few of the dummy eggs. If possible, allow her to walk quietly onto
the nest, closing the box behind her. If she is reluctant to enter
unaided, a gentle push should suffice, closing the door behind. Leave
the broodies to settle in their new environment for about one hour,
after which time a quiet inspection should be made. If they are seen
to be sitting on their dummy eggs, gently insert one hand under
the breast. This not only stimulates each bird to brood but helps
to accustom them further to being handled (see colour plate 1).

Should a broody be found standing in her box, a possible remedy
is to remove her to her tether, leave her for ten minutes or so to
feed and drink and then re-introduce her to the box. Repeat as necessary every couple of hours until dark. If still unsettled by the following morning, she should be returned to the flock. This is sometimes
a failing of first year birds.

Broodies are best fed on hard grain such as a mixture of whole
wheat and maize. Barley and oats are not recommended, nor are
pelleted feeds as these can cause the broody hen or bantam to produce very loose faeces which she may find difficult to hold for 24
hours. Any bird which is correctly fed but still fouls her nest during
her settling down period should be rejected.

The broodies should only be removed from their boxes once a
day for about ten minutes, usually around 10.00 am. This allows
them to feed, drink and most important of all, to defecate. It is very

Broodies should have ten minutes off their eggs each day to feed and defecate. Note that the coops are closed to help keep the eggs warm.

important that the broodies are removed from their boxes at the **same time every day and always in the same order**. This timing should only be interrupted in the case of very heavy rain; light showers make no difference to the birds, the timing being more important.

To remove a broody from her box, slide one hand under her breast and gently lift her upwards clear of the eggs, and out. Occasionally an old hen will pick up the odd egg under her wing, which can then drop and smash, so care should be taken when lifting the birds out. It is usual to tether the broodies when off the nest; left to roam freely they are extremely difficult to catch, thus wasting precious time. Tethering is done by using a trimmed, Y-shaped hazel or ash stick about 0.7m in length. Each stick is inserted into the mown ground opposite each box to form alternating rows. The first row should be about 0.5m from the boxes, with the same distance separating the two rows. The tethers are made from a good quality

106

cord such as butcher's string or braided nylon. A 0.6m length is doubled and then double knotted at one end to the stick, a sufficient distance being left between the knots to allow freedom of movement (see Figure 6). A loose loop is formed out of the main loop through which one leg can be inserted. The initial period of tethering can often witness the broodies flapping about and fighting. This further emphasises the importance of a three or four day acclimatisation period prior to the introduction of the real eggs.

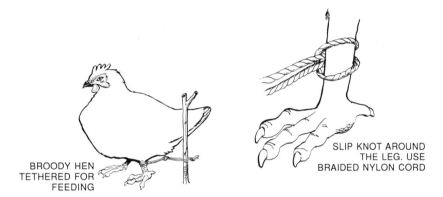

BROODY HEN TETHERED FOR FEEDING

SLIP KNOT AROUND THE LEG. USE BRAIDED NYLON CORD

Figure 6. Broody hen tethered for feeding.

Clean, fresh water must be provided for the tethered birds, together with about one good handful of mixed grain, normally placed between two birds in each row. Since the broodies are inactive, they will not necessarily eat all the food provided, particularly during the first couple of days. No bird should be returned to her box until she has emptied her bowels. If a bird is reluctant to empty herself, she may be stimulated by gently pushing her to and fro. During this settling down period, it does not matter if a bird is left off the dummy eggs for longer than ten minutes as there is, of course, no danger of chilling. Later on, whilst the broodies are tethered for feeding, the boxes should be closed to prevent excessive chilling of the eggs. This also helps the broodies concentrate on their feeding, as they cannot see their eggs. Once fed, each bird is picked up, the tether removed from her leg and the bird placed on the ground in front of her box and allowed to walk back in onto her nest. The tethers should be hung on their sticks and all droppings must be carefully collected using the small hand shovel and removed from the site. Should any droppings remain, the broodies' feet become increasingly soiled whilst feeding, thus transferring muck onto the incubating eggs and possibly introducing a risk of infection.

Setting and Incubating the Eggs

If the eggs are bought in, they should be given at least 12 hours to settle after the journey in a cool shed or building. At the time of purchase, check that they have been sanitised (washed in a germicide). Home produced eggs should be sanitised immediately after collection on a daily basis. It is worth pointing out that eggs which are to be incubated by broodies can be stored, if necessary, for approximately twice the time of those destined for artificial incubation, which is normally a period of seven days. All eggs should be stored in a cool, humid room with an even temperature of around 12–15°C (55–60°F). If stored on egg trays, the pointed end of the egg should be at the bottom. Whilst long storage is possible, best results are achieved from eggs which are three or four days old. Do not incubate eggs of widely differing ages under the same broody because staggered hatching may result. Nor should eggs straight from the laying pen be used, as some might not have had time to completely cool internally, which may again cause staggered hatching.

Once the broodies have completed their settlement period, the real eggs can be introduced. Firstly feed the broodies as normal, returning them to the dummy eggs. Once the feeding area has been cleaned and the birds have had a few minutes to settle, the real eggs can be introduced.

To introduce the eggs to the sitting birds, open one box at a time and remove all the dummy eggs from under the broody. Then replace these with the real eggs two to three at a time until the broody has received her quota. An average sized hen should comfortably take 20 pheasant eggs providing the nest has been made to the correct size and shape. Should any eggs be seen to be protruding out from the sides of the hen, one or two should be removed allowing the remainder to be correctly covered.

A few minutes should be allowed to enable each broody to settle on her clutch of eggs, after which time an extra egg or two can usually be placed under the bird. The final job in the setting of the eggs is to make a note as to the date each hen received her eggs. This simple chore is often forgotten and can be quickly done by chalking the date on the inside of each sitting box. Pieces of paper are easily lost!

Over the next 24 days of incubation, the eggs do not have to be manually turned. The broody will turn her eggs naturally each time she adjusts her position. It does no harm to give the eggs a gentle swirl with the fingers when lifting the broody out for her daily feed. Humidity is not usually a problem under broodies particularly when nesting on the ground, but during very hot dry weather it may benefit the eggs if the rearer flicks a small amount of clean water on to them when the broody is removed. If too much is used the eggs can chill.

Should any eggs be cracked or damaged during incubation, they should be removed but not replaced. Any good eggs that become soiled, either by broken egg or by an accidental fouling of the nest, should be cleaned using warm, lightly sanitised water. Any fouled nest material should be removed. If a broody's feet become fouled during feeding they should be wiped on the grass prior to the bird being returned to her box.

The normal incubation period for pheasant and grey partridge eggs is 24–25 days. Redlegged partridges have an incubation period which is 24–48 hours less. On the 22nd day the eggs should be carefully examined for signs of chipping at feeding time, even though this may not occur until the 23rd day. Chipping occurs when the chick is ready to leave the egg and is recognised by a small chip appearing approximately one third of the way down the egg from the rounded end. The morning after this is noticed, feed the broody as normal. On the morning after, do not lift her completely off the nest, but gently lift her front just enough to see the eggs. If there are signs of hatching and perhaps wet chicks visible, do not remove the bird for feeding. Re-close the box and check the remaining birds, removing only those where no hatching has occurred. The broodies with hatching chicks will come to no harm by not being fed. If they are removed, chick losses can occur through the broody trampling on the wet or partly hatched chicks as she returns onto the nest.

109

On the following day, usually the 24th, open the boxes and again lift the front of the broody. If hatching appears to have finished and dry, fluffy chicks are visible, allow the hen to re-settle on the chicks and shells. Remove one of the chicks from underneath her and place it beside her head. This is done to accustom the broody to the visual movements of the chicks. Do not be alarmed if she immediately pecks at the chick, but should she pick the chick up and bang it against the box in an attempt to kill it, great care should be taken with this particular bird in case she continues to attack and kill all her progeny. About 2% of broodies are prone to such attacks and they may eventually eat the chicks. If all seems well with the first chick, remove two or three more into her view and close the box. Once she has accepted her chicks, she should be lifted out of her box and tethered for feeding. Whilst feeding, the chicks should be collected up into a small box or bucket, ready to be taken to the rearing field. Any wet or late hatching chicks should be put under another bird with hatching chicks. Given good quality eggs, broodies will often return well over 90% of live chicks.

If a broody is found to be aggressive towards her chicks, tether her and allow her to feed. Return her to an empty nest, and once settled, re-introduce one or two of her chicks. It is usually only a matter of time before she becomes accustomed to the chicks. If aggression continues after an hour or so this bird should be rejected and her chicks shared amongst other broodies or given to a spare bird.

It is possible to buy in day old chicks and introduce them to broodies. In this case it is not necessary for the broody to have been sitting for the full incubation period. However, a minimum of ten days on dummy eggs should be allowed prior to chick introduction. The chicks should be introduced immediately after feeding. Two or three are placed under the broody once she has settled, allowing her to become accustomed to the feel of their movement. After ten minutes or so, bring one out and stand it beside her head for her to see. If all goes well with the initial chicks, introduce all of the brood. After 10 to 15 minutes in the box, remove all of them to the coop on the rearing field. Broodies with chicks should not be moved to the rearing field in the late evening, as insufficient light will be available for the chicks to imprint and find their foster mother.

110

Field Preparation for Broody Hens and Bantams

Having chosen and prepared the rearing field (as described in Guide No. 8, Gamebird Rearing), a final mowing and raking should have been completed a week before chick arrival. At least two days before their arrival, broody coops should be set close together without their runs, in a dry, sheltered corner. They should face away from the prevailing wind. In front of each coop enclose a nursery area of 1 metre square by erecting a 0.5m high surround of small mesh wire netting, supported by four sticks. The coop itself is a small floorless wooden box covering 0.6m square ground area. It is generally 0.5m high at the front and slopes to a 0.3m back; the centre panel in the roof slides forward giving access to the inside of the coop. The front is slatted as seen in Figure 7, with the centre slat being removable. A removable shutter is also required for the front, through which several 20mm ventilation holes have been drilled along its top edge.

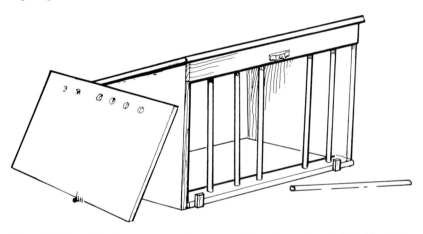

Figure 7. Coop displaying removable centre slat and coop board (used for shutting up at night).

Each coop should be supplied with one small feed dish partly filled with chick crumbs and a sprinkling of chick grit, and a drinker. The latter should only be a quarter filled with a mixture of water and vitamins and should contain a few pebbles in the lip to prevent

111

the small chicks from drowning. The food and water should be placed within the nursery area close to the front of the coop, thus enabling the broody to feed and drink. In wet weather the crumbs should be protected by using the coop shutter as a lean to. It is no longer desirable to feed the broody with grain. The chicks may attempt to eat it and choke.

The broody is first placed into the empty coop through the sliding roof and is given a minute or so to acclimatise to her new surroundings. Care must be taken not to chill the chicks during the transfer from sitting box to coop. Each broody in her coop should be given a maximum of 20 chicks, thus ensuring the equipment is used to its full capacity. If a shortfall of chicks occurs under home incubation, additional birds may be purchased and introduced to the broodies left in the sitting boxes. The chicks are placed on the ground inside the nursery pen in front of the coop and left to acclimatise and find their "mother".

Some broodies will immediately start to offer food to the chicks, whilst others will want to brood. It is not essential that the chicks feed or drink in the first 24 hours after their introduction to the coop as the remains of the yolk sac will be supplying their needs. In cold wet weather the coops should be checked after 15 minutes and any chicks seen to be chilling should be tucked under the broody's breast. For the remainder of the first day hourly checks should be made. If there is a danger from local magpies or crows, cover the nursery area with a piece of loose, soft netting to prevent them from stealing the chicks. In the evening of the first day the coop should be quietly closed so as not to disturb the broody and any stray chicks slipped under her. Once all coops have been closed, wait a short while. Should any chicks be heard to be whistling, quietly open up the coop top and slip them back under the broody. The coop should remain closed until around 7.00 am the following morning. At this time food and water should be replenished.

For the next two or three days the chicks should be checked several times a day and closed into the coop each evening. Any dead chicks should be removed. During this initial period it is not necessary to move the coop onto fresh ground.

On the fourth day, the chicks should be let out as usual for feeding and any remaining sitting broodies attended to. The broody is then removed through the sliding roof and placed into a crate or held by an assistant. The chicks are gathered and placed within a small box or bucket. The coop is then taken and attached to its run (see Figure 8) after which the nursery pen is no longer required. The feed dish and drinker, which should now contain water but no vitamins, should be placed in front of the coop, making sure at all times that the broody can reach them. The broody is returned to the coop and the chicks placed in the run. These runs are made from two standard 3m × 1.5m pen sections – one plain and one with a gate – together with two 'A' frame ends, one plain and one with a coop aperture (see Figure 8). The sections are tied together top and bottom, thus making a useful and easily moved small pen, which has many other uses in the rearing and releasing of gamebirds. (See Guides Nos. 8 and 10.)

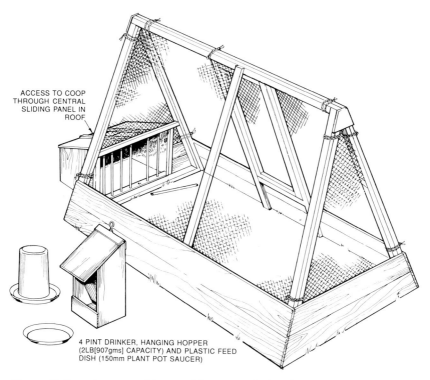

ACCESS TO COOP
THROUGH CENTRAL
SLIDING PANEL IN
ROOF

4 PINT DRINKER, HANGING HOPPER
(2LB[907gms] CAPACITY) AND PLASTIC FEED
DISH (150mm PLANT POT SAUCER)

Figure 8. Broody coop with movable run enclosing 3m × 1.5m ground area. (The coop is 0.6m square, the run 1.5m high.)

113

The chicks should be shut up each night until they are at least one week old after which, if the weather is fine and settled, they can be left unenclosed as they will have learned to return to the safety and warmth of the broody should they be disturbed. The coop and run should then be moved sideways on alternate days, to supply the birds with completely clean and fresh ground. This is best achieved by two people; care should be taken not to trap the chicks or their mother.

At around seven days there should be a 25% inclusion of mini pellets mixed among the starter crumbs. In the case of grey partridges such changes should be delayed for a further four to five days due to their smaller size. The birds should ideally be fed two or three times a day as time permits since full feed dishes result in excessive waste, particularly during wet weather. Birds should be allowed to clean up any scattered feed prior to replenishment of dishes. By 14 days the chicks are usually fed solely on mini pellets, with the small daily sprinkling of grit being increased to pullet size. Around the 14th day, given settled weather, the central slat can be removed from the front of the coop, allowing the broody access to the complete run. At this stage the food should be provided in a small hanging hopper, making sure it is hung low enough to enable small chicks to feed (see Figure 8), and the feed dish removed. Should just a feed dish be provided, the broody will cause excessive waste through scratching in the dish. Grit should now be provided on the ground and not through the hopper.

If a wet night is expected, it is wise to return the hen to the coop and secure the centre slat, as she might attempt to brood the young birds outside in the run. Should the rearer use a different style of pen where the coop is free-standing, care must be taken to prevent very young chicks from becoming trapped between the sides of the coop and the run. Once the broody has been allowed out of this free-standing coop, she should be returned and closed up each night to prevent her from roosting on top of the roof and thus causing the young birds to chill due to their inability to reach her. The broody, under this system, should continue to be closed within the coop at night, using the centre slat, until her brood is around three and a half weeks old.

At three and half weeks the food is gradually changed to growers pellets and the larger sized hen grit is supplied as necessary in a

114

small pile on a daily basis. While feather picking is not often experienced under this system of rearing, it is around this age when the first signs may occur. Should an outbreak be seen, all the birds should be beaktrimmed using an electric debeaker, or alternatively bitted using 'B' size bits, either plastic or metal depending on the rearer's choice (see Chapter 8). It is not necessary to beak trim or bit the broody as she will not be party to this vice.

At around five weeks some hens may begin to lay eggs. In some cases this can induce the broody to become very aggressive towards the poults. If she does not show any signs of aggression she can safely be left, but she should be removed if she is seen to attack the poults. No harm will come to the poults without a mother at this stage.

Due to the hardiness of gamebirds reared by using broodies, at five and a half weeks they can be released into the wild if necessary, and provided the weather is settled. Partridges would normally remain on the field until seven to eight weeks of age. For details on releasing broody-reared poults, see The Game Conservancy Advisory Guide No. 10, Gamebird Releasing (Published 1991).

CHAPTER TEN

Hygiene, Fumigation and Fogging

Clean and hygienic hatchery practice is second only to egg quality in importance for the production of quality chicks. In laboratories incubators are used to grow bacteria, so the risks of disease in unclean hatcheries are very high.

As a starting point a foot dip outside the hatchery building, which is replenished with a fresh mix as recommended, will help to reduce contamination. Similarly a bowl of hand sanitant inside the door which is used as a matter of routine will pay off in reducing contamination.

Sanitants

Disease microbes such as *Salmonella, E.coli, Aspergillus fumigatus, Mycoplasma* and rotavirus can cause loss in the hatching and the rearing units. Some may already be in the egg when laid, but others can quickly penetrate the porous shell. Besides these disease causing organisms there are others in the environment, eg. *Pseudomonas, Bacillus* and *Micrococcus*, which can also get into the eggs through the pores, causing embryonic loss even when present inside the egg in relatively small numbers. These eggs become "rots" and "bangers" and can readily spread further contamination to other eggs. Even before this there can be problems in the laying pens due to diseases like marble spleen disease, gapes, capillariasis and avian tuberculosis. Hence disease cannot be viewed in isolation from day-old production.

Effective practical hygiene makes economic sense in both the short and long term through reduced losses and healthier sturdy birds produced for rearing and release. Hygiene must not be neglected at any stage in gamebird production; it is an increasingly vital aspect now that so many birds are being intensively produced. There are many poultry disinfectants on the market which are suitable for use in game production, some of which have been tested specifically in the gamebird environment by the manufacturers.

As with any animal production, all equipment should be scrubbed and disinfected with the appropriate disinfectant and perhaps painted with a wood preservative before being stored away in a clean area. During use, feeders and drinkers should be regularly moved and kept clean and free of droppings, a source of much infection. Whenever possible a fresh area of ground should be used each year on a rotational basis.

The correct handling and cleaning of the egg will minimise bacterial, fungal and viral problems both in the incubator and in the rearing unit. Lower overall bacterial contamination will, for example, lead to fewer dead-in-shell.

The hatchery should have smooth non-porous surfaces throughout, including the floor, that can be washed and disinfected. Gloss paint or washable emulsions are easy to keep clean.

Since it is difficult to get into every nook and cranny to ensure that all dust is removed, the buildings, setters and hatchers can be fumigated or "fogged" with one of the modern oxidising disinfectants such as Virkon S. Fumigation using the old fashioned formaldehyde gas is not easy. The gas is highly noxious and the proper mask must be used and regulatory safety rules followed at all times. Containers must be very large relative to the volume of liquid, the building **completely** sealed, warm and damp, and a second person must always be present in case of accident. Entrances must be labelled stating that fumigation is in progress and no-one should enter the building. *Chlorine-based disinfectants* should not be allowed to mix with formalin or *formaldehyde gas as these mixtures can produce toxic fumes.*

Calculate the volume of the room/building and for every 28.5m³ measure out these amounts of chemicals.

Formalin   1.3 litres – maximum in any one container
Potassium Permanganate   850 grams.

They can be obtained from the local chemist who will be able to provide suitable measuring devices and advice on their handling.

117

IMPORTANT – *Formalin and the formaldehyde gas evolved from the formalin are very irritant to the skin, eyes and lungs, and contact must always be avoided.* Wash off any contamination with copious amounts of cold water. Wear rubber gloves, goggles and mask when handling the liquid. Ensure that the wind will blow the gas away from any house or farm building when the room is ventilated.

Close all the doors and windows, and block any holes. The air should be damp and warm but do not have any free-standing water or obvious wetness as this will absorb the gas and make it ineffective. It is essential that no gas is lost since a certain amount is needed for it to be effective. Porous and absorbent surfaces are difficult to fumigate.

First tip the permanganate into a very large metal or earthenware container of *at least* nine litres capacity. The sides should preferably slope outwards, never inwards. Place the container on the floor and quickly, but carefully, pour the formalin on to the permanganate. It is important that it should be done in this order. In a very short time a reaction will start. The last container should be by the exit door. Do not wait around, but leave at once and close the door tightly. Place the warning notice on the door and, if possible, lock it. After an hour, open up and turn on any fans to ventilate and disperse the formaldehyde gas. *Keep clear of the fumes!* If the correct proportions of the two chemicals have been used there will be a mound of brownish powder in the bottom of the container which can be washed out; but take care not to splash and stain the skin or clothes.

In addition to fumigating the building, it will pay to sterilise the setters and hatchers. Just before the first batch of eggs is set, fumigate the clean and empty setter. The amounts of chemicals required will be far less than for a room: a 1.4m³ setter will only need 65cm³ of formalin and 45g of permanganate. A wide shallow dish, about 50–80mm deep and 250mm wide is large enough to hold the chemicals. First get the setter warm, then fumigate for 30 minutes with the ports shut, and finally ventilate. A clean hatcher should be similarly dealt with; in many cases still smaller amounts of chemicals will be needed to match the size. Again, suitable measuring devices can be obtained from a chemist.

There are other occasions when fumigation is desirable. Following a hatch, there will be a great deal of contaminated debris in the machine which is difficult to remove without scattering some of it around. If the hatcher is first fumigated for an hour, any debris that is dispersed is less likely to contain live bacteria and fungal spores. After fumigation, the bulk of the debris can be removed and the interior and trays washed, disinfected and refumigated ready for the next batch. The remains on the table where the chicks were boxed are not so easy to deal with, but it can be damped down with a mild disinfectant before removal. A good quality industrial vacuum cleaner vented to the outside is useful to help to take up the fluff and small bits of shell.

Establishments should also fumigate the eggs in store and those recently set in the incubator. This should certainly be done for each batch, whatever the number of eggs, if there has been any history of salmonellosis. The chemicals are used as previously, but in the incubator the ports are partly shut and fumigation is carried out for only 20 minutes. It is important to first bring the new eggs up to temperature for a few hours before fumigation – no water should be present in the trays. Eggs that have been set for 24–96 hours, pipped eggs and chicks should not be fumigated. Means to rapidly ventilate the fumigated machine must be provided. The manufacturers of incubators may suggest an amount of formalin to suit their machine.

Disinfectants have recently been developed which are an improvement on older types, especially those which have a highly virucidal activity and can be used to fog a hatchery, for example Virkon S. In this case a fogging machine is required. In general these disinfectants are less noxious than fumigants and much easier to handle. It is not necessary to seal all the holes in a building, but fogging can be continued until the fog is seen coming out from the holes.

"Custom hatching", that is moving eggs from one, two or more different laying units to a hatchery elsewhere, and sending the chicks back to the estate providing the eggs or to yet other estates, greatly increases the risk of disease being disseminated between estates, the more so as the number of sources of eggs increases. *Salmonella* is often spread in this way to estates originally free of salmonellosis. More significantly, this system poses a threat in relation to viral diseases, several of which are becoming more common.

Where custom hatching is used it is vital to ensure as high a standard of hygiene as possible. This means that the hatchery should

119

check that the eggs come from a flock of known high health standards. The laying unit must carry out meticulous egg sanitation, boxing the eggs for transport in disinfected and fogged boxes. They should be transported in a clean, disinfected vehicle and the eggs resanitised on arrival at the hatchery. The egg boxes must be destroyed or disinfected if returned to the egg supplier.

Disinfectants

Effective disinfection is not simple and a number of points must be remembered. Disinfectants are **aids** to good sanitation.

Disinfection is not instantaneous and takes time to kill microbes. Disinfectants may have a restricted range of activity, some being better for bacteria, some for viruses and so on. Some work poorly in the presence of organic matter such as droppings, while others are better in this respect. The active ingredient in a solution is used up during the cleaning process so do not expect a solution to do more than it is capable of. Cleaning and the removal of contaminated matter from a surface, such as the wall of an incubator, is as important as the use of a disinfectant. The two go hand in hand and the use of fresh solutions at the correct temperature will help sterilise a surface. A disinfectant cannot always penetrate deeply into a large lump of debris and has to be assisted by brushing and scraping. Some types tend to combine with debris to form a layer on the lump, stopping further penetration. Overnight soaking of equipment with dried on lumps, and such porous objects as wooden hatching trays, will allow much easier cleaning. A suitable disinfectant solution should be used for this.

There are three broad groups of disinfectants, many of the products based on them having detergent or cleaning properties to help remove the solids.

1) Phenolic based types
2) Iodine/chlorine based types
3) Oxygen based types

The first group functions best where there is a lot of organic debris, such as droppings or yolk, present on a surface. When a surface

120

is reasonably clean then the iodine/chlorine types can play an effective role. The oxygen types, such as Virkon S, are generally less toxic and can often be used to fog a unit, as well as being useful as general disinfectants. Buckets used for disinfectants should be labelled as such and never used for food or water for livestock.

Emphasis has been laid on the buildings and equipment, but microbes can be easily spread to' eggs and chicks from people's hands, which should therefore be washed with soap and dipped in a hand sanitant both before and after handling eggs and equipment (see p. 92). It is worth noting that large commercial poultry units check their staff for the presence of *Salmonella* before allowing them to work in the unit.

Disease

To be able to produce good numbers of eggs and healthy day-olds, a bird for egg laying or incubation must be free of infection and disease. Birds can act as carriers infecting the egg yet showing no signs of disease.

Disease can be kept to a minimum by choosing healthy birds and maintaining clean conditions.

Avian tuberculosis is virtually always present at a low frequency in any flock, but where the same ground is used year after year and stocked with second year and older birds the risk of this disease is high, with losses occurring particularly in late winter and summer. Besides the loss of birds, the flock will be less productive. There is no treatment for this disease and control is achieved by using clean land, young rather than old birds and, where relevant, penning birds off the ground. Also any bird that has lost condition at any time of the year should be culled and the body burnt as a matter of course. Where there are heavy losses consideration should be given to a total cull, or whole-blood testing for the disease and culling, then restocking fresh land with new young birds. It must be remembered that the bacterium can survive in the soil for very long periods – a year or more. However, exposure to sunlight by working the ground is helpful in reducing contamination.

Where there is a history of salmonellosis no survivors should ever be used as stockbirds, even if treated, as there will be a few carriers left to infect some eggs and the ultimate hatch. Tagging survivors will ensure that none will be used for egg production.

Viral disease cannot be treated and it is probably best, where practicable, to avoid eggs from survivors of an outbreak. In some instances hens that survived may transfer a protective antibody to the egg and hence to the chick. It is only likely to last a few weeks, but often this is sufficient to get the chick past the critical period. Discuss the problem with the veterinary surgeon "in charge" of your birds. Whatever course of action is decided on, egg sanitation and handling must be of a very high standard. For the future, in the lifetime of this edition it is possible that one or more vaccines will become available to prevent certain viral diseases, if sufficient funding is made available for research into the manufacture and necessary licensing of such products.

CHAPTER ELEVEN

Gamebird Autopsies and Therapy

Information obtained in cases of loss and ill-health from independent laboratory post-mortem examinations and tests is relayed to the veterinary surgeon "in-charge" of your birds, as he is the person legally required to make an assessment based on his knowledge and examination of the flock and any supporting studies at his own or other laboratory, and ultimately he must advise the client as to a course of action in terms of therapy, relevant husbandry and management. He will also issue any prescriptions and advise on whatever drug usage he considers necessary. These drugs are frequently in the POM (Prescription Only Medicine) category, and can be obtained only from a veterinary surgeon or pharmacist.

Besides POM, some drugs belong to another legal status category known as PML (Pharmacy and Agricultural Merchant List). These do not require a prescription for normal use but do require a prescription if the mode and rate of use or species to be treated, eg. pheasant, partridge, etc, is *not* given on the data sheet. This is a designated document specifying the nature of the drug and its intended licensed use as a direct therapeutic agent or, as is often the case, as a feed additive.

PML drugs, even when intended for the specified uses given on the data sheet, may be purchased in unopened packages, for large numbers of birds, from those companies trading as agricultural merchants who are registered with the Royal Pharmaceutical Society of Great Britain, or from veterinary surgeons and pharmacists. If small numbers of birds are involved, the basic manufacturers' package can be split before sale *only* by a veterinary surgeon or pharmacist. Where PML drugs are incorporated as a feed additive, purchasing will be in the hands of the feed compounder, whether commercial or private. Also the user of PML drugs, whether they are in the form of a direct therapy product or already present in compounded feed, has to be a *bona-fide producer* of gamebirds and must *not* sell, supply or hand over any drug product or medicated feed to any other person or use it in unlisted species.

Where animals or birds are intended for human consumption, the withdrawal period must be complied with. This means that in the context of game shooting, the period between the *end* of treatment and shooting must be at least as long as the stated withdrawl period recorded on the product label. Under normal circumstances shoots which follow the Code of Good Shooting Practice will exceed this by a considerable margin.

Regulations and Directives are being produced regularly by the EC and national governments and it is impossible to give full details in this book. The Game Conservancy may be contacted for information about the latest developments in the law on any aspect of game production.

Whenever there is doubt as to the cause of death or poor hatch, consult the vet "in-charge" of your flock.

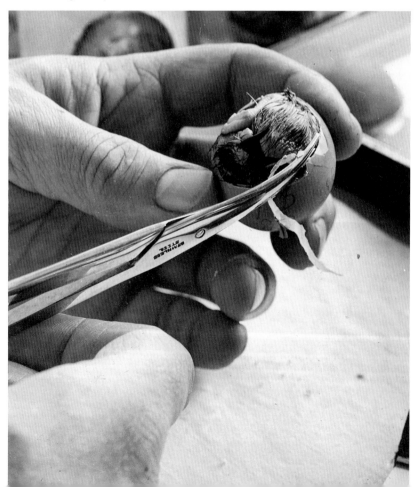

CHAPTER TWELVE

Egg Production and Hatchery Records

Good, consistent records are well worth the time and effort involved to help pinpoint the causes of poor production, to plan remedies and to improve an average unit. Where The Game Conservancy has advised on an incubation problem, it has been a great help to be able to go back over several years' records and assess the long term norm and variation in the unit for comparison with the current year.

The main records should include:

(a) Daily egg production in each pen.

(b) Daily maximum and minimum temperature and humidity of egg store, setter and hatcher room.

(c) Daily wet-bulb thermometer reading in cabinet machines.

(d) Weight loss of set eggs.

(e) Aperture size on still-airs.

(f) Hatching results.

(g) General daily notes on egg production and incubation, eg food, disease problems, adjustments to incubators and chick quality.

Examples of recording charts are given in Figures 9–11 and may be modified to suit local circumstances.

From these records it is possible to know if egg production and storage have been normal; whether the humidity in the incubator was correct in relation to the air-space, especially if adjustments had been made, and whether the fertility and hatchability levels were satisfactory. If anything unusual was recorded it may be possible to associate this with a change in, for example, the number of eggs laid or their hatchability, and then to correct it for improved quality and production.

Figure 9. WATER REGIME AND AIR SPACE DEVELOPMENT

| S/TIME | WET BULB OF | WATER ADDED | TRAY | | WEIGHTS | | | | % WT. LOSS | |
			No.	DATE SET	EGGS & TRAY	TRAY	EGGS	LOSS	ACTUAL	EXPECTED

Figure 10. EGG PRODUCTION

	SPECIES			WEEK BEGINNING			
PEN.	**DAY**						
	THURS.	FRI.	SAT.	SUN.	MON.	TUES.	WED.

Figure 11. HATCHER ENVIRONMENT

Date	Time	EGG STORE			SETTER ROOM			HATCHER ROOM		
		Min°C	Max°C	%RH	Min°C	Max°C	%RH	Min°C	Max°C	%RH

127

APPENDIX A

Mains or Equipment Failures

A mains failure alarm in the keeper's house is considered essential. In the case of a short term power cut there is probably little to worry about. In theory turning, temperature and ventilation must all be maintained. But turning can be allowed to lapse for a few hours without dramatic effect. Some loss of heat is also sustainable, especially if the eggs are well developed and producing a fair amount of their own metabolic heat.

There can be a strong temptation to close down ventilation to maintain heat, but this can cause an excessive build-up of carbon dioxide and result in the suffocation of embryos. It is better not to close the vents.

If a portable generator is not available to supply power as needed, or if the breakdown is of the machine rather than the power source, extra heat can be provided by standing a large sealed can of hot water in the bottom of the incubator. This may be all that is needed while repairs are carried out.

Even apparently severely chilled eggs *may* survive. Do not abandon them in the event of a breakdown or accidental switching off of the machine.

APPENDIX B

Incubation Defects

There are many reasons why incubation is not always successful, and even experts often find it difficult to pinpoint the crucial and contributory reasons. There are few easily identifiable defects, but the causes of some problems are indicated below. A correction can then be tried. A record of the defect and its frequency is useful when formulating advice.

Defect	**Probable causes**
1. Many "clears" (ie infertiles and very early deads)	Infertile cocks Poor diet Eggs stored too long and under wrong conditions
2. Blood rings inside shell	Temperature too high or low Incorrect fumigation
3. Many dead-in-shell	Incorrect temperature Incorrect turning Incorrect humidity
4. Pipped eggs not hatching	Insufficient humidity in hatcher
5. Hatching too soon, too late or sticky chicks	Incorrect temperature, especially too high cut-off temperature
6. Uneven hatch	Eggs too diverse in age
7. Malformed chicks	Temperature incorrect Incorrect setting and turning
8. Deformed chicks	Specific dietary deficiencies

9.	Small weak chicks	Eggs too small Too low humidity in setter
10.	Spraddling chicks	Hatching trays and take-off box too smooth
11.	Heavy breathing chicks	Disease Too much fumigant left in hatcher Too little air movement once hatch virtually complete
12.	Mushy chicks – (rapid post-mortem decomposition)	Low average temperature Contaminated incubator High humidity in setter Poor hygiene

A Short Guide to Sources of Equipment and Materials

As there are many manufacturers, backed by extensive networks of agents, the following list of sources of equipment and materials cannot pretend to be complete, but it should provide a primary guide from which to start looking for suitable pieces of equipment or materials for your hatchery. The full address is given when the firm is *first* mentioned.

In addition game farms and agricultural companies, while supplying more general shoot items, often stock what is specifically needed by a hatchery and the egg production unit and trading with the local firm may save time and costs. These names and addresses are not listed here but can be found in the current Trade Directory and Advisory Guides produced by The Game Conservancy and in the general press. If, however, equipment or materials cannot be obtained in your area, then the manufacturer or agent should be approached. In case of particular difficulty The Game Conservancy will always be pleased to advise, as will The Game Farmers Association.

The Game Conservancy has gained considerable experience in the use of a number of different items over the years and the manufacturer or main agent in this country for any such product is marked with an asterisk*. The absence of the asterisk simply means that while we are aware that the article or group of articles is available, we have not had the opportunity to carry out usage trials; use does not necessarily indicate approval. The Game Conservancy is always looking for new and improved products and is prepared to consider trials in collaboration with the manufacturers.

Incubators, setters, hatchers and fittings (Manufacturers)

A B Incubators*
40 Old Market Street, Mendlesham, Suffolk IP14 5SA
Tel: 0449 766065, after hours 0449 766471 **Fax**: 0449 766065

Brinsea*
Brinsea Products Ltd, Station Road, Sandford, Avon BS19 5RA
Tel: 0934 823039 **Fax**: 0934 820250

Bristol Incubators & Hatchers*
Patrick Pinker (Game Farm) Ltd, Latteridge, Iron Acton,
Bristol BS17 1TY
Tel: 0454 22 416

Buckeye
Lopen Group Ltd, Mill Lane, Lopen, South Petherton, Somerset
Tel: 0460 41310 **Fax**: 0460 42063
Tel: 0452 29455 **Fax**: 0621 742680

Eltex*
George H Elt Ltd, Eltex Works, Bromyard Road, Worcester
Tel: 0905 422377 **Fax**: 0905 421892

Funki
A/S, Kirkevænget 5, Hammerum, DK-7400, Herning, DENMARK
Tel: 97 11 60 44 **Fax**: 45 97 11 81 62

Grumbach
Brutgeräte Gmbh & Co KG, PF 170041, D-6330,
Wetzlar-Münchholzhausen, WEST GERMANY
Tel: 06441 72039 **Fax**: 06441 72890

Hamer*
Hamer Incubators, Bradshaw, Bolton, Lancs BL2 4JP
Tel: 0204 852555 (Spares only)

Hardwick/Maplin
Hardwick Game Farms, Horsecroft, Bury St Edmunds,
Suffolk IP29 5NY
Tel: 0284 754611

Jennings Cabinet Incubators
A E Jennings, Iron Cross, Salford Priors, Nr Evesham,
Worcs WR11 5SH
Tel: 0386 870321

Marcon*
Marcon Game Stock Ltd, Flaxton, York YO6 7PZ
Tel: 0904 86588

Mayfair
Mayfair Incubators, Churt, Surrey GU10 2QS
Tel: Headley Down 712264

PAS Reform
Bovensdorpstraat 11, PO Box 2, 7038 ZG Zeddam, HOLLAND

Petersime
Petersime nv, Centrumstraat 125 – B, 9870 Zulte (Olsene)
BELGIUM
Tel: 091 88 9611 **Fax**: 091 88 8458

Vision
Sunrise Agricultural Engineers, 60 Bateman Road, Hellaby,
Rotherham, South Yorkshire
Tel: 0709 545619

Victoria
Via Lardirago 4, 27199 Pavia, ITALY
Tel: 0382 467271/467272 **Fax**: 0382 467271

Western*
Lopen Group Ltd, Mill Lane, Lopen, South Petherton, Somerset
Tel: 0460 41310 **Fax**: 0460 42063

Spares for modern incubators

These can normally be obtained from the manufacturers, their
agents, appointed service engineers or some game farms.

Spares for obsolete machines

Such machines as Glevum, Gloucester, Hearson, Ironclad, Secura and Eyles are not currently manufactured, and spare parts cannot be obtained from the addresses found on the machines or operation manuals. The following companies may be approached for equivalent spares, in addition to a number of game farms.

Incubator Specialists, Toledo Works, 81 Hollis Croft, Sheffield **Tel**: 0742 700651

Patrick Pinker (Game Farm) Ltd

S Young & Sons (Misterton) Ltd, Crewkerne, Somerset TA18 8NU **Tel**: 0460 34361

In case of difficulty The Game Conservancy will suggest where parts might be obtained if the usual supply has dried up and can advise on the operation of obsolete machines. Operation manuals can sometimes be supplied.

Candlers

A E Jennings*

Patrick Pinker (Game Farm) Ltd*

Western Incubators

Egg washing equipment, chemicals and measuring apparatus

Local game farms, agricultural suppliers, pharmacists and horticulturalists.

Antec A H International Ltd, Windham Road, Sudbury, Suffolk* **Tel**: 0787 77305
Egg sanitiser and disinfectants

134

Pitman-Moore, Crewe Hall, Crewe, Cheshire CW1 1UB
Tel: 0270 580131 **Fax**: 0270 589804

Paper, Chemical & General Ltd, Old Vicarage Drive, Appleby, Scunthorpe, South Humberside DN15 0BY
Tel: 0724 732101/734025 **Fax**: 0724 734802

SWC Health & Hygiene, India Road, Gloucester, GL1 4DR

Vantec Ltd, Market Drayton, Salop*
Tel: Market Drayton 2303
Egg washer

Balances

Salter* – See Yellow Pages

Game Farmers Association

Oddington Lodge, Moreton-in-Marsh, Glos GL56 0UR
Tel: 0451 30655

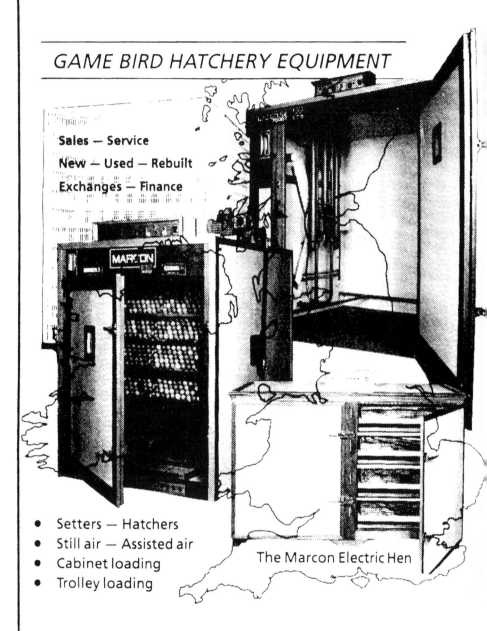

Sportsman
Game Feeds

A complete range of high quality pheasant and partridge feeds

Formulated and manufactured to the highest quality standards these feeds contain a high plane of protein nutrition for the early stages of growth in order to produce sturdy, well-feathered birds resistant to disease and chilling. Sportsman Game Feeds are available nationwide and are fully supported by nutritional advice and after sales service.

Slimbridge
Wildfowl Feeds

A comprehensive range of feeds ... suitable for all types of waterfowl, and formulated to meet the requirements of The Wildfowl Trust at Slimbridge.

Particular attention has been paid to the nutritional demands of waterfowl to ensure high fertility and hatchability during the breeding season, followed by strong growth and good feathering of young birds without excessive weight gain.

For further information contact
Sporting Feeds, 3A West Market Place, Cirencester, Gloucestershire GL7 2NJ
Telephone: (0285) 658884 Fax:(0285) 651038

A Department of J. Bibby Agriculture Limited.

A.B. MULTILIFE RANGE
OF SETTERS AND HATCHERS
For the Small Shoot or Estate.

All our Setters are Moving Air Type machines, with fully automatic turning, electronic humidity and temperature control, in both the General purpose and Game Setter models as standard.
All Hatchers are also Moving Air Type machines, with automatic electronic humidity control.

A.B. MULTILIFE 1500 MK2. GAME SETTER.

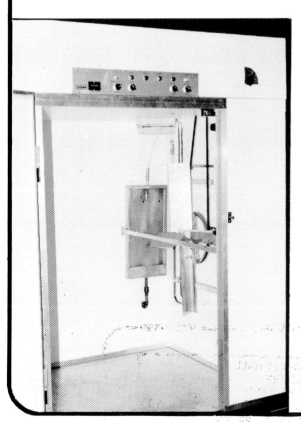

GAMEKEEPA FEEDS LTD

INCUBATOR KITS (excl. Cabinet)
25, 50, 75 or 100 egg size

70 egg Incubators

BRINSEA INCUBATOR RANGE

ELECTRIC CONVERSION FOR GLEVUM

New and used Western, Bristol and other makes of Incubators
and Hatcher usually available

Spares for most Incubators.

Pheasant and Partridge egg size

INCUBATOR EGG INSERTS

Rotomaid Egg Washers and all spares

GAMESAN EGG WASH POWDER

QUALITY BREEDERS PELLETS

MAIL ORDER CATALOGUE AVAILABLE

THE GAME
CONSERVANCY

**SOUTHERLY PARK, BINTON
STRATFORD-UPON-AVON,
WARKS. CV37 9TU
BIDFORD (0789) 772429
FAX (0789) 490536**

TRADE MEMBER

PONTELAND
NORTHUMBERLAND NE20 0AQ
TEL: 01661 880808

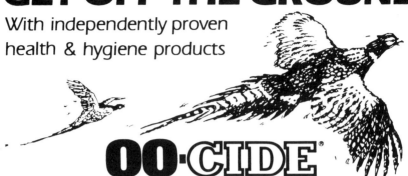